OFFICES AT WORK

OFFICES AT WORK

Uncommon Workspace Strategies that Add Value and Improve Performance

Franklin Becker

Foreword by Tom Kelley

JOSSEY-BASS
A Wiley Imprint
www.josseybass.com

Published by Jossey-Bass
A Wiley Imprint
989 Market Street, San Francisco, CA 94103-1741   www.josseybass.com

Jossey-Bass books and products are available through most bookstores. To contact Jossey-Bass directly call
our Customer Care Department within the U.S. at 800-956-7739, outside the U.S. at 317-572-3986 or
fax 317-572-4002.

Jossey-Bass also publishes its books in a variety of electronic formats. Some content that appears in print may
not be available in electronic books.

Library of Congress Cataloging-in-Publication Data

Becker, Franklin D.
        Offices at work: uncommon workspace strategies that add value and improve performance /
Franklin Becker; foreword by Tom Kelley.—1st ed.
        p. cm.—(The Jossey-Bass business & management series)
        Includes bibliographical references and index.
        ISBN 0-7879-7330-0 (alk. paper)
        1. Office layout. 2. Performance. I. Title. II. Series.
        HF5547.2.B38 2004
        658.2'3—dc22
        2004012069

Printed in the United States of America
FIRST EDITION
HB Printing   10 9 8 7 6 5 4 3 2 1

CONTENTS

PART TWO: GUIDELINES FOR IMPLEMENTATION   109

FOREWORD

Readers old enough to remember the original *Star Trek* television series may recall Capt. James T. Kirk in his booming voice at the beginning of every episode declaring space as "the final frontier." The venerable Captain Kirk dedicated his life to the *outer* space of galaxies far away; Frank Becker has spent most of his career exploring the frontiers of *inner* space in office environments here on earth, where most of us nonastronauts spend our working days. Although the twentieth century seems to work pretty well on *Star Trek*, a quick tour of twenty-first-century offices suggests that there is still plenty of room for improvement in the present day.

Building on the insights from his previous book, *Workplace by Design* (coauthored with colleague Fritz Steele), Becker has done a systematic analysis of the opportunities and pitfalls encountered in optimizing workplaces for effective teams. Though we have a long road ahead of us, Becker helps light the way.

Given that there are so many things to get right in running a successful organization, is managing office space the most powerful tool in a manager's toolbox? Certainly not. But from my experience, it is one of the most underused, which is why the issue of office space is still somewhat of a frontier. "People," as executives have been fond of saying for the past fifty years, "are our most important asset"—not to mention the single biggest expense for most enterprises. But even though many businesses have increasingly sophisticated systems to measure and motivate their *people,* most organizations seem much less strategic in the way they deal with what is probably their second greatest expense: office space.

In fact, what I have noticed is that managers—even otherwise enlightened managers—are implicitly or explicitly asking the office space question in a certain utilitarian way. They are essentially saying "What is the quickest, cheapest way I can get all four thousand of my people a desk, a chair, and a wastebasket?" Asking the question this way assumes that space is some kind of threshold variable, like the supply of water or electricity, in which quality is assumed to be equal (above some minimum safety specification), and once you have enough quantity then more is not better. On the contrary, suggests Becker, space can be quite strategic. I couldn't agree more.

With *Offices at Work,* Franklin Becker gives a wake-up call to businesses around the world. So dive right into Chapter One and seek new answers (even where you may not have been asking questions) to the challenges of optimizing office space for your twenty-first-century enterprise. There are rewards to be gained by fine-tuning your office environment. Far from being a mere utility, space can be a strategic tool that influences the attitude and behavior and even the performance of your space. Focusing attention on the final frontier of inner space will be time well spent.

Tom Kelley

ACKNOWLEDGMENTS

As is true with any body of work conducted over a period of years, many people have contributed in ways large and small to my thinking, experience, research, and consulting over the years. My colleague Bill Sims, with whom I have worked for almost twenty-five years now at Cornell University, continues to be someone whose views and insights I seek out and value. Bill and another friend and mentor of even longer standing, Bob Sommer, have subtly but pervasively influenced the book, and more broadly my career.

I am deeply indebted to the many people who took the time to read early drafts of the manuscript and provide invaluable feedback: Pat and Rex Barnes, Alan Drake, Linda Gasser, Lenny Nissensen, Tom Osmond, Art Pearce, Bill Sims, and the students in my graduate seminar at Cornell. This book would have been impossible without the editorial assistance of Paul Cohen, with his wonderful ability to quickly slice through rough-hewn material and help me shape it into a coherent story. My editor at Jossey-Bass, Kathe Sweeney, made this book possible with her enthusiastic support for this book from beginning to end.

Finally, there would be nothing to write about if it were not for the companies with which I have had the privilege to consult over the years, and the organizations and their Cornell University IWSP representatives who have supported and participated in the International Workplace Studies Program research for the past fifteen years. To all of these people, my heartfelt thanks and appreciation.

OFFICES AT WORK

INTRODUCTION

Every organization (and every employee) performs a bit better or worse because of the planning, design, and management of its physical workspace. Decisions about whether to have an open floor plan or closed offices, how to size and furnish offices and public spaces, whether to co-locate facilities on a campus or disperse them regionally, whether even to have assigned office space for every employee, all affect employee satisfaction and productivity.

It is a realm where unintended consequences loom large. In the age of the knowledge worker, where information, collaboration, and innovation are decisive, a workspace redesign that saves a hundred dollars per employee but impedes interaction can be disastrous. Given the financial stakes (for most companies, facilities represent the second largest expense after payroll), every manager, starting with the CEO and including those in facilities, corporate real estate, operations, and human resources, should understand the dynamics of the physical workspace. This book, I hope, enhances that understanding.

The influence of space on behavior is not always obvious, but it underlies many social and organizational puzzles. I've been intrigued by this connection most of my life. I grew up in Sacramento, California, and as an undergraduate I attended the University of California at Davis. On return visits to Sacramento I became interested in how the building and design in Sacramento of one of the new generation of pedestrian malls was working. These were intended to revitalize tired and dispirited downtown shopping districts that were being eclipsed by glossy new suburban shopping centers with acres upon acres of free parking. But the new Sacramento Mall didn't seem to be contributing much to the revitalization of downtown. So I started to study it.

I observed pedestrian behavior and interviewed merchants and city officials, including the city planners responsible for its redesign. In short order, I learned that the merchants and city officials attributed the limited commercial success of the mall to the "bums" on the mall and in a nearby city park. Politicians and planners believed these men were frightening away the desired middle-class shoppers. I found this odd, since my pedestrian counts of people on the mall, categorized by age, gender, and other demographic factors, revealed only a tiny number of people who might be described as bums. More prevalent were retired working-class men, mostly Mexican. The city planners lumped them all together as "undesirables."

They believed that if they removed these old men from the park, middle-class shoppers would park in greater numbers in the covered parking garage adjacent to the park and feel less frightened cutting across the park to get to the Sacramento Mall. The redesign worked to a certain extent; the old men did move on. The problem was that they moved on to the mall. Then, of course, they were considered a problem there. So actions were taken to eliminate them from *that* area. The redesign of the park, and then parts of the mall, set in motion for these working-class men a kind of demographic forced march around Sacramento's city center and beyond. The city planners thought of each of these places as pretty much unrelated to each other. In fact (to use a phrase I wouldn't invent for another thirty years), they were part of a series of loosely coupled settings.

Putting Knowledge to Work

As the Sacramento example demonstrates, actions, designs, and behavior in one place influence these same factors in other places. The endgame isn't just laying bare underlying planning goals and values, or describing their impact on the behavior patterns of groups of people. It's translating this information into principles for better practice. Sacramento's planning approach shifted the problem from one part of the city to another. Why not instead provide amenities that the retired gentlemen would appreciate—comfortable places to play checkers, get out of the sun or rain, or have a cup of coffee—close to where they lived, and where they would choose to congregate? Placed thoughtfully, activity magnets of this kind zone both space and the people attracted to them in ways that separate incompatible activities without resorting to direct barriers.

Thirty years later this approach is finally taking root with another group of citizens we often if not exactly fear at least would rather just see disappear: teenagers. Today, cities are building skateboard parks because they know a segment of the teenage population is naturally drawn to them. It's a case of spending money on design informed by an understanding of what various segments of the population care about and use and appreciate. Not a bad model for a city, or the workplace. My interest in workspace was shaped by this ecosystems perspective. Taking the time to understand how underlying social and organizational systems influence, and are influenced by, the physical settings in which we work puts knowledge in our hands. Resources are invested where they make a difference.

My colleague Fritz Steele and I coined the term *organizational ecology* to capture this dynamic, interdependent view of the places where we work.[1] The alternative offices we saw in the early 1990s interested us because they were highly diverse places that recognized and accommodated, even celebrated, the value of giving people lots of choice in where and when and how they worked. These workspaces succeeded because they accomplished more, doing better, with fewer resources. The last thing we imagined was that alternative offices would morph into a dull, gray, uniform landscape designed to chop out costs in the name of "flexible" working.

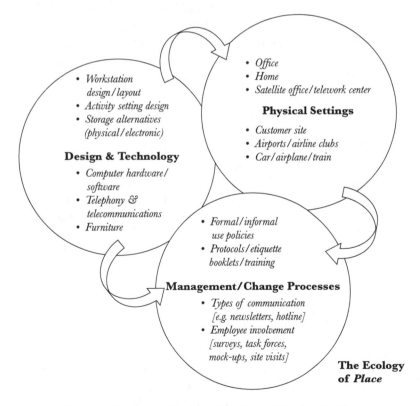

Figure I.1. Organizational ecology: The basis of an
integrated workplace strategy.

Smart Offices Work on Many Levels

Consider what has happened to "hoteling," the idea that office space would be available to people as needed rather than permanently assigned to one individual (see Chapter Five for details). Giving up ownership of a Dilbertlike cube, or even a "real" office with four walls and a door, seemed to me ten years ago—and still does today—a pretty good deal *under certain circumstances.* Those circumstances include being able to work whenever and wherever you feel you would be most productive, inside or outside the office. You might not "own" your office, but whatever space you use would be *better* than what you might have been allocated on an individual basis. This approach generates costs savings, and smart companies reinvest these savings in higher-quality shared work areas and more and better amenities and technology.

For me, the model was offices like those of SOL and the former Digital Equipment Corporation in Finland. Almost a decade before the concept of the dot com surfaced, porch swing sets, leather recliner chairs, the sound of water splashing in decorative fountains, brightly painted wall murals, plants, and free food redefined the concept of a corporate office in these and other leading-edge companies. The driving force wasn't to be hip. Sales and performance exceeded expectations, corporate branding skyrocketed from lavish and positive media attention, and bright people wanted to come to work in these companies. They were also cost-effective. Real estate costs were reduced by about 30 percent because having some unassigned offices meant less space was needed overall. That such novel solutions are limited to a relative handful of companies—mostly dating to a burst of innovation in the early 1990s—speaks volumes about how far we have to go to realize the promise of the well-designed workspace. The fact is, few companies have moved beyond fad and fashion to diffuse new workspace-design strategies (whether from other industries and regions or distant corners of their own organization) throughout their business. Many researchers have investigated such failures to innovate (see for instance *The Knowing-Doing Gap,* by Jeffrey Pfeffer and Robert Sutton).[2] My hope is that by better understanding the values, principles, and logic underlying effective workspaces, executives can more systematically implement them.

One Size Doesn't Fit All

No single workspace solution is perfect. Accountants, human resource professionals, and marketing specialists are not cut from identical molds. Computer programmers from Minnesota don't have the same workstyles as their counterparts from India and China. Today for the most part we stuff them all into the same work environment and tell them to get on with it. It may work in the military, where discipline and uniformity serve a serious and evident purpose. But accounting firms, pharmaceutical companies, banks, and hundreds of other types of businesses face divergent pressures and need more varied solutions.

Diversity in workstyles and workspaces, from workstation to building portfolio, strengthens a company's competitive advantage by giving it a more multifaceted set of solutions for dealing with a highly unpredictable business environment. This kind of ecodiversity goes against the grain of standardization and universal planning which is the bedrock for workspace design strategies in most large organizations today. It reflects, however, current thinking in biology about the value of biodiversity. The greatest threat to a species over time, and to an ecological system, is the absence of a rich and diverse gene pool.

Demonstrating a simple, direct, and precise connection between a complex ecology and range of subtle organizational outcomes is difficult. Yet companies that invest in their workspace not as a real estate asset but as an organizational asset know that space that is well planned, designed, and managed energizes employees, improves morale, and contributes to the social relationships and interaction patterns that underpin all knowledge work, even in today's increasingly digital world. That's what this book is about. It succeeds if it casts some light on vexing questions that every organization, large or small, must consider in convening itself in space and time:

- *Uncertainty.* Business in the twenty-first century is fraught with ambiguity, doubt, and risk. This uncertainty extends to brick-and-mortar issues of space planning, and to related issues of corporate identity and loyalty.
- *Diversity.* Executives must a strike a balance between standardization—which reduces costs and creates consistency—and variation, which supports individual strengths, local needs, and flexible responses.
- *Goal clarity.* To use scarce resources to their highest potential, decision makers must know what really counts for the organization, in the short run and the long run. Yet the strategic goals of the organization often get lost when it comes to planning and managing workspace.
- *Systems thinking.* Everything about the workplace—social, cultural, and physical— is interconnected. Changes in one area often have unexpected effects elsewhere in the system.
- *Performance management.* Managers often look only at short-term costs or savings associated with a facility. Broader measures of performance are necessary to understand how the workspace adds value throughout the enterprise, from its impact on people's efficiency and effectiveness to living the brand to attracting and retaining the best and brightest staff.

As they tackle such questions amid a constellation of competitive pressures, organizations are forced to fundamentally rethink every aspect of their business model, including design and use of the workspace. Ultimately, this pressure can be reduced to a simple imperative: do more, better, with less. To do so, companies over the past decade have embraced a variety of *workspace strategies* designed to change work patterns, attitudes, or performance through changes in the physical workspace, from the layout of a floor to the location, design, and use of an entire building or campus.

Each of the chapters that follow addresses a particular workspace challenge—what mathematician Horst Riddle called "wicked problems" because they have no simple solutions. Throughout the book I identify the key ideas central to the chapter by displaying them in this type. Part One of the book, "Principles of Workspace Design," is intended as an operator's manual for understanding core issues of workspace strategy and performance.

> Chapter One, "The Office as Invention," looks at how managers shape the workplace, for better or worse, through their own assumptions about the nature of work.
>
> Chapter Two, "Knowledge Networks," gives a brief history of the office and shows how offices can better serve a knowledge-based economy.
>
> Chapter Three, "Co-Location," examines the ups and downs of proximity, whether across the hall, the parking lot, or the region.
>
> Chapter Four, "The Right Size," considers the impact of physical scale on community and performance.
>
> Chapter Five, "Mobility," assesses the perks and pitfalls of remote working and explains the crucial differences between mobile and virtual work.
>
> Chapter Six, "Flexibility," is a guide to designing and building space that meets the fast-changing needs of organizations.

Part Two, "Guidelines for Implementation," tackles problems of another order: developing, measuring, and managing a new workspace strategy.

> Chapter Seven, "Getting Started," suggests ways to assess an organization's real workspace needs—and the effectiveness of its workspace fixes.
>
> Chapter Eight, "Workspace Planning Tools," reviews powerful analytical programs that help managers gather information and define their goals and assumptions.
>
> Chapter Nine, "Measuring Performance," suggests how to assess an organization's real workspace needs and the effectiveness of its workspace fixes.

Chapter Ten, "Managing Workspace Change," presents tools and techniques for planning and implementing new workspace strategies.

Chapter Eleven, "The Value of Uncommon Sense," offers some counter-intuitive lessons about effective workspace design and lays out ten simple rules for improving workspace performance.

My goal is not so much to advocate for a particular workspace solution as to reveal the underlying workplace ecology that creates the conditions for failure or success *over time*. Corporate leaders responsible for helping shape the workplace reside at all levels and in every part of the organization, from finance and human resources to marketing, real estate, and facilities management. Whether they are formally labeled "workspace strategist" or not, my hope is that the intellectual fire that comes from challenging commonly accepted working assumptions will forge a new mind-set about the role that workspace can play in improving organizational performance.

PART ONE

PRINCIPLES OF
WORKSPACE DESIGN

CHAPTER ONE

THE OFFICE AS INVENTION

The office is as it is today because that's how we imagined it yesterday.

The office isn't God-given. It's an invention. We can change it. Changes are often forced by circumstances: the need to expand or consolidate operations; a strategic shift to new products, activities, or regions; a merger or acquisition. In other cases, workspace changes are driven less by objective physical requirements than by a CEO's desire to shake up the status quo, promote new ways of working, or make a statement about the organization and what it values. But any change of workspace, whether a move to a new building or reconfiguration of a single department, can have enormous impact on the life of an organization and its people. For most of us who work in offices, few things are as tangible and emotionally charged as the physical setting in which we operate.

The office as we know it today has evolved in response to particular expectations, activities, technologies, economic conditions, worker demographics, and social values. We may attribute decisions about a company's workspace to a tidy world of functionality, but life is more complicated. Much of current office design is justified by untested assumptions and unstated values. Is it really so obvious that co-locating everyone on a corporate campus improves communication and collaboration across business units? Or that an open plan environment is unsuitable for jobs requiring a high level of concentration?

Send the Intended Message

The workplace is not always what it seems. It doesn't always work the way we think, or wish it did. Like any good story, it's as much a product of our aspirations and imagination—and our fears and anxieties—as our rationality. Workspace design can convey, more clearly than we might desire, just what we value. The physical cues of the office send environmental messages. Some are intentional, some not. We pay attention to physical cues precisely because they seem less consciously controlled than verbal expressions such as a mission statement or corporate values statement. I have never found an organization, for example, that proudly proclaimed, "People are *not* our most important asset." But I've found lots of offices sending that message unintentionally through mean and dingy "break rooms" and floors the size of a football field packed with identical workstations.

Draw on the Past to Reinvent the Future

Innovation in the places where we work, like the cars we drive, is shaped by the fact that the past exists in the present and the edge influences the center. Today's family car, equipped with rack-and-pinion steering, antilock brakes, and aluminum and graphite panels and parts originated in race cars and jet fighters. The modern home-based telecommuter has something in common with a thirteenth-century monk who worked from "home." The suburban house with the office above the garage shares lineage with the neighborhood shop over which the proprietor and his family lived. Peter Drucker argues that if you want to predict the future, look around you today.[1] Whether it's to build an innovative place to work, or innovative products and services, managers must observe and understand the world around them.

Raise Your Aspirations

As we embark on the twenty-first century, at least in the developed countries, the sweatshop has been replaced for the most part with bright, clean, and comfortable space. Rarely do contemporary offices endanger our health on a daily basis. Few of the places where we do office work horrify us; occasionally they energize us. Typically, they simply bore us to tears. As individuals, and organizations, we don't have to make such a stark choice. We don't, because the office as we know it as an invention, and like any other invention it can be reinvented. By designing our offices with imagination and grounding the design in an understanding of the ecology of work and workers, we can do better than create places that (as Florence Nightingale advocated for hospitals) do no harm. We need to raise our aspirations.

Minimally, where we work should be part of a healthy ecosystem in which we as individuals, teams, and organizations can not just survive or be productive but flourish. Yet when I ask friends, students, and colleagues about their image of an ideal place to work, it's like opening a faucet with low pressure: a little stream of ideas quickly peters out. Ask them about their ideal home and it's like opening a fire hydrant: complex images and stories pour out in an endless stream of energy and enthusiasm. Given how much time we spend working, there's no good rationale for the places where we work to engender such a barren mindscape.

The answer isn't likely to be found in high-tech gizmos. How many of us are excited by a future that offers sensors that automatically control lighting and temperature, adjust our chairs, and turn on and off green and red lights to let others know when they can approach? Does this kind of technoworld inspire passion, enthusiasm, or commitment? The effort millions of employees spend personalizing their workstation with photos of children, dogs, their summer vacation, and sports and entertainment celebrities suggests a desire for something more than functionality in the place they work, no matter how whiz bang it may be.

Exploit Disequilibrium

We need to understand the context in which our organizations operate, but it isn't necessary to flash-freeze an older and more familiar world, or try to tame the unruly one we live in today. Forces for disequilibrium abound—among the foremost information technology, which continues to transform our everyday lives. The invention of the telegraph, and then the telephone at the beginning of the last century, accelerated enormously our ability to communicate at a distance. Cellular telephones, pagers, and the Internet seemingly eliminate the barriers of time and space. We can work from anywhere and everywhere, easily accessing an astonishing amount of information. But how we plan, design, and manage the place where we work needs to catch up with how we actually perform our work. Frank Duffy argues that although there has been a renaissance in organization theory, "the design of the vast majority of office buildings has stayed physically more or less exactly where office design began."[2] With the possible exception of Northern Europe, Duffy writes, "Facilities managers share with architects and designers a great deal of responsibility for what is, by any standard, an astonishing case of conservativism."

Why Is Workspace Change So Slow?

The slow pace of change in how we plan, design, and manage our workspace, Frank Duffy argues, stems from managers' still believing that:

- Workers have to be constantly supervised.
- Advances up the organizational hierarchy must be marked with more space and better furniture.
- Departments and functions should be kept separated.
- Quasi-monopolies should control information flow.
- "Presenteeism" is better than "absenteeism."
- Home and work are two irreconcilable worlds; commuting is the natural state of mankind.

We all live in the twenty-first century, but many organizations continue to inhabit a nineteenth-century mind-set about work and the workplace. Despite shattering advances in technology and our attitude about family, work, and society, these older and often unstated values lurk just beneath the surface of organizational life. Like a submerged wreck that gouges holes in the hulls of unsuspecting passing ships, these time-worn values retard progress. In Duffy's words:

> In the age of the Internet, at the dawn of the knowledge-based society, it is strange that we tolerate buildings . . . that assume that everyone comes in at nine and leaves at five, and sits solidly at a desk for five days a week. The model, of course, is still the factory where foremen had to put enormous emphasis on synchrony to force a barely literate proletariat to work at the loom and the lathe. When the bell rings the work begins. When the siren blows it is over—for the day . . . rolling out formulaic solutions has become the norm in office design.

Organizational leaders with a nineteenth-century mind-set contribute to dulling the advance of new, healthier, more engaging, and more mobile ways of working. There is disparity, however, among what is technically possible with modern telecommunications, what people care about, what makes them effective in doing their work, and what motivates downright resistance to change of any sort. We need to separate surface from substratum if we want to identify what fails because it fundamentally undermines the ability to work productively (in which case failure serves a valuable purpose) and what generates resistance because it challenges the familiar. What wins out over time is whatever demonstrably works better than what came before it.

In a Global Economy, Scan the Globe

In a global economy, lessons about what works better can come from anywhere. Long before American office planners realized the advantages of "universal plan" (same-size) offices for managing employee churn, the Swedes gave the same-sized office to virtually every employee. They did it by inventing what they called the "combi office." To gain the quiet of a closed office and the high visibility and transparency associated with an open office, the combi office combined a standard-size cellular (closed) office of about one hundred square feet with a sliding glass door. The Swedes did this not because of research demonstrating that sitting in an office with real walls, near an operable window and natural daylight, or having beautifully designed furniture, increased productivity a few percentage points. The idea that every aspect of the environment must be justified by direct utility or efficiency is peculiarly American.

Rather, the Swedes did it because offering a beautiful, comfortable office was considered the right (decent) thing to do in a society that values the dignity of its workers. I can still remember my slack-jawed astonishment the first time a Swedish manager wondered aloud why I would even question the practice of assigning a secretary the same space as an engineer or human resource manager. "Don't they all contribute to the organization's success?" he asked me. If they did, why would you give anyone a demonstrably lower-quality working environment for no reason other than to distinguish rank and status? "Wouldn't this undermine their morale and commitment to the organization?" he persisted.

Swedish offices succeed at many levels. We've adopted them in the form of the universal plan office because they use space efficiently. The same-size office reduces the cost of churn because it's easy to move people in, out, and around the organization rather than move walls or panels to accommodate these changes over time. Small but uniformly sized offices distribute space more evenly across the organizational hierarchy than the space-by-rank approach, which can easily result in something like 40 percent of the employees occupying 60 percent of the space. An added bonus of the more egalitarian approach is the environmental message that the corporate leadership considers everyone in the organization valuable, not just its higher-level managers.

Leverage Benefits; Succeed on Multiple Levels

As with Scandinavian offices that are beautiful, functional, and cost-effective, the challenge is to create a workspace ecosystem that functions on multiple levels, from the individual and team to the organization as a whole. IDEO, a firm renowned for its ability to develop category-busting new products (such as the design for the Palm Pilot), does just that. The office feels more like a play space than a workspace, but that's because play is so critical to creative thinking.[3] It's hard to think outside the box when you're in one. IDEO's offices generate lots of interest because they are so different. They contribute to the brand and to public visibility. But they also help attract the best and brightest talent, without which the company could never succeed. Once at work, talent is encouraged by the space to share ideas, to interact freely and often. The space is flexible and costs less than would a high-end, more conventional corporate environment. Design, values, work processes, marketing, and learning reinforce each other and work in harmony. IDEO's leadership leverages every facet of the workplace because they understand and pay attention to how the whole ecosystem works, not to just a few selected parts.

Leverage Workspace Solutions

High-performance workspace strategies succeed on many levels at once. Each benefit leverages another.

- Cost
- Flexibility
- Branding
- Attraction and retention
- Teaming and collaboration

Nurture the Organization

Getting an organization's ecology right is like planning a garden. Gardeners don't plant rhododendron in the sun, sunflowers in the shade, or roses in the swampy bit of the garden in the expectation that they will "just get on with it." They select plants that thrive under the conditions the garden affords. By exploiting the garden's natural variations, they create a diverse, healthy, sustainable plant community, one that over time gets better and better. Good gardeners constantly experiment. They place plants in a number of locations, in varying combinations. They observe the result, and if it doesn't work, they replant, reorganize, and replace. They graft to create new varieties. The old resides with the new, and it is the overall pattern—the landscape, not the individual plant—that creates the total effect. A good office, like a good garden, requires tending. On its own it will go to seed, become overgrown, and finally perish.

Ultimately, the offices we invent are shaped by an intricate web of relationships; events; and financial, technical, and human factors interpreted in light of individual, professional, corporate, and societal values and attitudes. Aligned and in harmony, the organization, like the garden, flourishes. A workspace strategy at odds with other organizational values, policies, and practices wastes time, money, and energy. What works isn't always what common sense might suggest.

Benchmark the Whole System

Invariably, what works depends on the organizational context. That's why, as managers develop new workspace strategies, they must beware of a popular business tool: benchmarking. Following the lead of others can yield disastrous results. It is not that we shouldn't try to learn from others' experience. Rather, it is that we need to understand the particular ecological system within which a given strategy succeeds. In the case of workspace, this means understanding not just the workstation design but the organizational culture, management and employment policies and practices, and the nature of the work and workers.

Avoid Benchmarking Traps

When you learn about what other admired companies are doing, also understand the context in which their particular policies and practices exist. Consider:

- Organizational culture
- Workforce demographics
- Technological sophistication
- Regulatory environment
- Market forces
- Stability or uncertainty of operating conditions

Embrace Paradox

As John Naisbitt and Patricia Aburdene argued more than a decade ago[4] and others have done more recently, a more fruitful approach than trying to ignore or suppress complexity lies in both-and rather than either-or thinking and solutions. It's what I call "complementary opposites." The Chinese call it yin and yang. We don't have to choose between what appear to be diametrically opposed points on a spectrum: decentralization or centralization, standardization or choice, individual or team. Harness both to improve performance. Take the layout of offices. Selecting a single modular furniture system standardizes purchasing across the corporation and benefits from discounts associated with national contracts. Yet units within the firm—and even teams and groups within a unit—can arrange the furniture to suit their own workstyles and work processes. The key is first to select a furniture system that employees themselves can reconfigure with genuine ease. Second, and equally important, managers must encourage individuals and groups to manipulate their work environment because it is one of the most direct and visible means a company has at its disposal to demonstrate that it trusts employees and will give them the tools they need to work productively.

We frame decisions in terms of either-or choices in part because the alternative seems to make the world more complex. In a corporate world where people feel over-taxed and underresourced, any proposition that appears to make the daily world more complex isn't going to win many hearts and minds. A mind-shift is needed, one accepting that simplicity sometimes comes with and benefits from variety and choice, not at its expense. Embracing paradox can take less energy and generate more motivation than pretending it doesn't exist or trying to suppress it. Healthy ecosystems require and thrive on diversity. Think of workspace as you would a financial portfolio: never put all your eggs in one basket. Good advice for your financial investments; so too for your workspace strategy.

Implications for Practice

- Start significant workspace interventions by analyzing existing and emerging trends in work processes, organizational culture, workforce demographics, and information technologies. Identify business challenges, which can range from potential merger and acquisition to shifting market, political, and economic conditions.
- Don't assume current workspace solutions must be working because there is no dramatic failure evident. Workspace solutions are rarely life-threatening, but they can cause the four D's: significant disruption, dysfunction, discomfort, and dissatisfaction.
- Create project teams that involve people in the planning and design process, including architects and designers who have not specialized in office planning and design. They are more likely to think of fresh solutions because they are not so grounded in what constitutes "good" (as in: familiar) office design.
- Balance what's possible with what's feasible. The whole organization's workspace strategy doesn't need to change in one fell swoop (and rarely does). It advances incrementally, even though some of the small steps may feel like radical change at first.

CHAPTER TWO

KNOWLEDGE NETWORKS

Getting to know someone using e-mail goes only so far. At some point you need to actually meet the person you think you've fallen in love with.

Few would doubt as we embark on the twenty-first century that knowledge is a company's most important resource. It is the fuel that feeds the engine of innovation and steadies the business in a turbulent environment. Getting the right people is necessary but insufficient. What's needed are the right people continuously learning, sharing information and ideas, and challenging each other. Yet we neglect the physical context in which learning (and with learning, leadership) *always* unfolds. How do I supervise or mentor people I rarely see, even if we both sit within a hundred feet of each other? Where exactly do new hires learn to do their job and tap the experience of old hands—while in turn teaching more experienced workers about new technology, methodologies, and mind-sets? In successful organizations, significant learning happens every day, formally and informally, throughout the workplace. This is why the office environment, and the extent to which it is open or closed, still makes so much difference. Access to electronic databases is useful, but as Valdis Krebs writes: "An organization's real edge in the marketplace is often found in complex, context-sensitive, knowledge which is difficult, if not often impossible to codify and store in ones and zeroes. This core knowledge is found in individuals, communities of interest and their connections. An organization's data is found in its computer systems, but a company's intelligence is found in its biological and social systems."[1]

The choices an organization makes about the ecology of the workplace and about how space is allocated and designed directly and indirectly shape the infrastructure of knowledge networks—the dense and richly veined social systems that help people learn faster and engage more deeply in the work of the organization. We know that knowledge networks govern how and to whom information flows, and at what speed, and that this influences performance as well as innovation. Cultivation of knowledge networks underpins the continuing debate about office design, and the relative virtue of open versus closed offices. The debate is vociferous, but it is argued mostly with personal opinions formed by experience with a limited number of workplace strategies.

The Evolving Office

Like the lesser panda, advocates of the open plan office exist, but actual sightings among rank-and-file staff are rather rare. This is odd, really, when you realize that for most of economic history open offices *of some sort* have predominated. From the Great Halls of manor homes in the Middle Ages until after the first third or so of the twentieth century, most workers doing office work did it in a shared room. Looking at photos from the Lloyds Bank archives in London from around the turn of the twentieth century, you see pictures of crowded, dingy, poorly lit attic rooms full of properly dressed young clerks sitting and standing among piles of paper. Photos of senior bank managers in the same period show comfortable surroundings with better furnishings, lighting, and carpets, but they too occupy shared rooms (albeit with four to six rather than twenty to thirty or more colleagues). In these early offices partners often sat facing each other across doublewide "partners' desks," making it hard to keep secrets and easy to know much of what was going on. These were in many ways the kind of team-oriented office we strive for today, albeit far less tidy and comfortable and with much more paper. No one might have heard of a "knowledge network," but it flourished.

Rediscovering Work as a Social Activity

Open plan thrives today in part because of the associated space efficiency. But companies are also rediscovering the office as a social setting. What goes on in the office—why we have offices—is not terribly different from what went on in offices we have known for the past hundred years or so. The work is similar: people labor individually and in groups, they store and access files, they use technology, they socialize, they have meetings. The office is a place where people come together to engage in activities that help the enterprise persevere and prosper.

The primary difference from early offices is that over a hundred years the idea of the office as a social setting got lost or at least diminished. We can fault Frederick Taylor and *The Principles of Scientific Management* [2] for that. It was Taylor who, in the name of efficiency, broke down complex tasks into discrete, repetitive activities that could be done quickly by people with little training or skill (and because of that, at lower wages).

Taylor's work led to constant surveillance and strict management control of workers. Out of this climate emerged a management view that socializing was a waste of the corporation's time. Being on task was what counted.

People came together in increasingly large purpose-built office buildings, especially as the twentieth century wore on, because that was where specialized equipment was (initially typewriters, telephones, and mimeograph machines, and then computers, copiers, printers, and fax machines). But they also continued to come together to meet, share information, and socialize, and for supervision. It was only in the late 1950s and early 1960s that one began to see widespread use of panels to create a private (one-person) environment for staff up and down the organizational hierarchy. For the first time, organizations created places where rank-and-file staff were expected to work alone, to be productive and "focused." In effect, the panels replaced supervisors, since the physical barrier made it harder to socialize. It also, of course, made it harder to get to know your coworkers or your boss, or to share information and ideas without making a physical effort to interact.

The panels permitted minimal acoustic privacy, but they did define rather precisely one's own turf. As has been the case in human history, the size and location of one's territory began to mark distinction in status and rank. Higher-ranking people got larger cubicles and higher panels. The highest-ranking people got real walls and doors, with the size of the office reflecting their relative standing among the corporation's elite.

The office, which began largely as a social setting, evolved into one that more closely resembled a factory floor for physically isolated human machines. Over the course of a hundred years the focus on groups of people working together (not always as a team, but rarely physically separated as individuals) shifted to an environment designed to support and reinforce individual performance.

That individual focus and the associated physical model have come into question over the last decade as industries ranging from insurance and banking to technology and pharmaceuticals increasingly have relied on teams to solve complex problems requiring expertise from multiple disciplines or departments. Interaction and communication—the office as a social setting—has once again emerged as a primary purpose for coming together in a place called an office.

Recognizing the Way We Work

Few people work in total isolation. Even jobs such as financial analyst, which we have historically viewed as requiring a high level of concentration (and the associated private, closed office), are beginning to change. A year ago I interviewed the director of research for one of the world's leading financial services company. By company policy he was entitled to a large private office and a $50,000 budget for furnishing it to his satisfaction. I found him sitting in the midst of his team in an open plan workstation. He explained that retreating to a private enclave to reflect on data for days, and then writing a considered report, just didn't cut it any more. To be competitive, he and his team had to frequently interact and share information, making rapid judgments that exploited fast-changing and unpredictable market events. Forcing him to occupy a private office was tantamount to involuntary incarceration in an intellectual prison cell.

Advances in technology have further shifted the focus of the office to the social aspects of productive work processes and the knowledge networks supporting them. We can access information from virtually anywhere, anytime, with modems and other high-speed connections. We are not absolutely dependent, and will be even less so by the end of the first decade of the twenty-first century, on information stored in file cabinets or desk drawers in a place called the office to be able to carry out our individual daily tasks. Our homes are, on the whole, larger and increasingly connected to the Internet and corporate intranets. It is far more feasible to work from home today than it was a hundred or fifty—or even five—years ago.

Working at home is technically feasible, but research consistently shows that few people want to work at home full-time, five days a week. We want to come in to the office several times a week, not because it has specialized equipment or there is insufficient space at home, but because we miss the camaraderie and social interaction—the buzz—of the office. By some estimates middle managers spend more than 80 percent of their time in oral communication. This figure is even higher for upper-level managers. Most of this communication involves face-to-face interaction.

These activities do not imply socializing as opposed to working, but socializing in all its forms as the work itself. Conversation and social interaction, rather than being wasted time that must be discouraged, are the bedrock of collaboration and team effectiveness.[3] Productive and satisfying social relationships are a major reason for coming into the office every morning. Many conversations could be (and many are) easily handled by telephone or e-mail. But electronic communication doesn't substitute for getting together face-to-face occasionally. Embedded in the social camaraderie of the office are the building blocks of productive work processes: the opportunity for building trust, tacit learning and mentoring, getting and giving clear direction and timely feedback about ongoing projects, learning how the organization works in practice and not in theory.

Providing Space for Continuous Learning

Learning springs from many sources. Formal training and written texts play a role, but informal conversations, observations, experience, and personal insight—what has been called tacit knowledge—constitute the richest source of knowledge in most organizations. As Ronald Mascitelli describes it: "Tacit knowledge lies below the surface of conscious thought and is accumulated through a lifetime of experience, experimentation, perception, and learning by doing. It is rooted in personal experience, and is often filtered through one's own perspective, beliefs, and value structure."[4] The propagation of tacit knowledge is dependent on relationships and communication. Tacit learning occurs in a serendipitous, unplanned way, as a by-product of our routine, daily activities. It is learning that depends on being able to see and hear and observe how others handle various situations.

Planned, scheduled meetings facilitate coordination within and across teams and units. They're useful, but much of this can be done today using electronic communication. Much less amenable to electronic communication is the kind of tacit learning that underlies and characterizes an effective work relationship. It is the difference between sitting in a conference or training room attending a two-day training seminar led by a designated expert and what happens every day observing someone who handles irate clients well or has a terrific way of framing a sales pitch. The distinction is important because, as John Brown and Paul Duguid argue, how people actually work differs fundamentally from how organizations describe that work in manuals, training programs, organizational charts, and job descriptions.[5]

Supporting Communities of Practice

It is through an informal community of peers that employees learn how to navigate the corporate bureaucracy, who to contact for the most accurate information, what the undocumented tricks are to making a program work, how to best approach a certain type of client, and so on. But the exchange of such information and insight is not automatic. Learning, according to Lave and Wenger's concept of legitimate peripheral participation, involves becoming an "insider."[6] This suggests that it is not abstract knowledge of the work that is needed for learning but participation in the real-world practices and informal communities in which that knowledge takes form.

Communities of practice and the tacit learning that occurs in them depend ultimately not on bureaucracy's rules, programs, and manuals but on personal trust, which comes from knowing people sufficiently well to make informed judgments about their intentions and character. Individuals have an easier time getting access to information essential to doing their job well once they are trusted by their group members.[7]

How Open Plans Affect Learning

A work environment that is open facilitates informal, tacit learning because it creates opportunities for interaction. A computer engineer captured this perfectly: "As you are [working], you are picking things up from hopefully everybody you're working with. You're working with them because they bring other talents to the table. So when I'm listening to how other people are working on deals or business negotiations, not only am I working on mine, but I'm learning how they're doing it."[8]

But what do we mean by a "more open" environment? Most people, if asked to describe an open office, depict some form of office cubicle, the ubiquitous "cube" made famous in Scott Adams's Dilbert cartoons. With its walls formed by one to four panels anywhere from three to seven feet high, the office cube has been described as a "rabbit warren" because of the confusing maze that results when dozens if not hundreds of virtually identical boxes occupy a floor.

Missing from the open versus closed debate are distinctions about the particular type of open plan office. Describing a work environment as open serves little purpose. It is like using *car* for everything from a Ford Escort to a Bentley Corniche. It's correct, but learning that some people hate driving and others love it means little without knowing which kind of car each group has driven. The same holds true for understanding people's reactions to open office environments. To appreciate the impact of our design choices on work performance, it's important to first understand the forms of open space and then see how knowledge flows in each type of space.

The Bullpen

The endless rows of desks facing a platform for supervisors found at the turn of the twentieth century in such famous buildings as the Larkin Building in Buffalo, New York, and Frank Lloyd Wright's Johnson's Wax Building in Racine, Wisconsin, were truly open. Unlike earlier workspace that more closely resembled a factory than what we have come to know as an office, these "cathedrals of commerce" celebrated light and openness and so were a distinct improvement on their predecessors. But organizationally, they were designed to eliminate rather than encourage communication and interaction. These huge undifferentiated rooms with hundreds of neatly ordered desks came to be known as a "bullpen." Like the rabbit warren, this was hardly a flattering metaphor. It captured the idea of animals milling around, easily observed and controlled, penned up, with no place to go.

Bureaulandschaft: Office Landscape

Originating in Germany in the late 1950s as the *bureaulandschaft* (or "office landscape"), the open plan office was intended to physically reflect and enhance the flow of communication. Like the industrial plant, the office was viewed as a place where raw material entered (data) and was processed in an orderly fashion to create a product (a report, presentation, proposal). This led to use of freestanding panels that could be easily and quickly repositioned to reflect changes in a team or work process. This new form of work process efficiency carried with it the philosophy of industrial democracy, with its emphasis on reducing, if not eliminating, hierarchy. Without walls and doors impeding the flow of information, decisions could be faster and more collegially. Requiring less space than closed offices, office landscaping seemed to offer the best of all worlds. It didn't. After a brief fling, most Northern European companies discarded the concept. Vast expanses of undifferentiated workstations grated on the European sensibility, which valued community and what the Germans call *Gemütlichkeit,* a kind of friendly sociability, over raw efficiency. It took only a little longer for Americans to abandon office landscaping, but for their own reasons.

Despite its egalitarian rhetoric and ethos, the United States was not ready to allocate space in a way that undermined status and hierarchy. Giving everyone, from the youngest accountant to a seasoned manager, offices of the same size diminished the differences between those who planned and managed and decided things and those who carried out these decisions. Managers (many of whom at senior levels retained their closed offices) liked the space savings associated with panel-based furniture systems, and the concept that they were easy and inexpensive to reposition as the organization evolved. They also liked status and hierarchy, so they married the two in the unlikely form of the cubicle.

Integrated Furniture Systems: The Cube

The office landscape came to the United States first in Rochester, New York, at Kodak's world headquarters. From the beginning, its reception in the United States was lukewarm. Individuals who had worked in closed offices complained about noise and disruption, lamenting the disappearance of wide variation in office size and furnishings to mark differences in status and rank. At about the same time, Robert Probst, the brilliant head of design at the furniture company Herman Miller, introduced the Action Office furniture system. It too substituted moveable panels for fixed walls, but the panels were now a structural element in an integrated system rather than a freestanding furniture system. Desks became "work surfaces." They were hung off vertical panels, along with storage bins and shelves. With the exception of seating, freestanding furniture was replaced by integrated furniture elements that yielded the requisite structural rigidity by being bolted together with ingenious fastening systems. Efficiency in space use was increased by removing cabinets from the floor and exploiting airspace by hanging them on the panels.

Americans adopted the panel-based furniture system concept, but without the underpinning of industrial democracy. Workplace standards specified differing office size and varying types and quality of furniture and accessories for employees categorized into three, four, five, or more grades. As employees were promoted they might move from a 6' × 6' workstation with panels on two sides to one the same size with more panels. With further advancement they might occupy a 6' × 8' or 8' × 10' workstation with higher panels on four sides. With promotion and a larger workstation came more expensive materials. Wood edges or a wood top replaced Formica and steel work surfaces. Carpets graced bare floors, and a blue carpet might be upgraded to red. What had begun in Germany as a concept for improving the flow of information was transformed in the United States into one in which space efficiency was overlaid with the countervailing weight of status and hierarchy.

Although integrated systems furniture reduced significantly the amount of space per person required and could be reconfigured without tearing down and physically destroying conventionally constructed walls, the flexibility came at a steep price. Despite being "demountable," the cubicle was far less flexible than its conceptual progenitor, the *Bureaulandschaft* office landscaping. Special tools and expertise were needed to disconnect and reconfigure the new integrated systems furniture. Individual workers or managers could no longer reposition a desk themselves as they had in the original landscaped office, or for that matter in the conventional office room. To top it off, a kind of domino effect was introduced, since changing any one workstation triggered changes in all those connected to it. In major office installations, this could affect hundreds of workstations. The facility manager for a global financial services company in London

**Rows upon rows of cubicles afford little acoustic privacy and
inhibit rather than promote free flow of communication.**

The panel-based integrated workstation's efficiency comes from using vertical surfaces for storage and from the ability to reduce office size without creating the claustrophobia that the same-size office with full height walls would.

reported recently that a single change in office configuration triggered five hundred workstation moves. This same company spent $50 million annually reconfiguring space in its New York offices alone. The International Facility Management Association, which tracks statistics on office churn in the United States, reports that it's not unusual for companies to turn over 50–100 percent of their office space in a year.[9]

Furthermore, opportunities for tacit learning and the free flow of information were undermined rather than strengthened by the integrated panel system. Panel-based workstations keep people focused on their individual task and reflect the predominant view for most of the twentieth century that conversation, particularly of a social nature, is off task and a waste of time. The physical panel did the job of the corporate drill sergeant, keeping everyone focused on his or her individual task.

Workspace and the Flow of Knowledge

Office workers hate cubes. This isn't surprising. Cubes don't do anything well except reduce the amount of space required per employee compared to a closed office with floor-to-ceiling walls. The 6' × 8' cubicle, or even a 6' × 6', can be found in profusion

**We humans are adaptable, but no office environment should be designed
that tests the limits of ingenuity just to hold a quick conversation.**

in hundreds of companies. It may be cramped, but we recognize it as an office. From
another perspective, we do build 6' × 8' and 6' × 6' rooms, but we call them cells, not
offices, and they are as likely to be occupied by criminals or monks as software engineers and human resource professionals.

Employees toiling in a warren of identical panel-based workstations have consistently and vociferously complained that lots of interaction and communication
per se doesn't equate to effective or valued communication, or productive behavior for
the whole team. Yes, informal communication is integral to productive work. Available research suggests, for example, that:

- Many lesser decisions and much of the coordination during execution of a project
  get done in brief and opportunistic encounters. Unintended meetings are as frequent as scheduled meetings, yet on a per-meeting basis they take only one-third
  as much time to accomplish.[10]

- Conversation of all kinds gives some opportunity to enjoy the company of coworkers, learn more about them, and build bonds with them. By contrast, scheduled meetings fulfill these needs inefficiently, occur less frequently, and take more time.[11]
- More than 80 percent of observed work-related conversations are unplanned.[12]

The challenge is to develop workspace solutions that balance the need for meaningful interaction with the opportunity to work without distraction.

The Team-Oriented Cluster

It's easy to see why managers tasked with reducing costs really like cubicles, and why employees concerned with personal and professional identity as well as their individual productivity don't. This is usually where the debate about open versus closed offices ends. But the panel-based office cubicle is just *one form of open plan office solution.* Open, small-scale team-oriented clusters of twelve to fifteen workstations without panels can do more than cubicles to promote the meaningful communication and trust on which knowledge networks and tacit learning depend. What is counterintuitive is that the more open environment can also reduce unwanted distraction and interruption.

Thinking Beyond Partitions

An office built around a cluster of a dozen or so freestanding workstations not separated by panels captures an unanticipated benefit of having more rather than less openness: access to nonverbal cues. In office cubicles you cannot ask your neighbor a question, or even see what she is working on, without somehow interrupting her—by walking around, peering over, or calling through the adjoining panel. In a team-oriented cluster where the small group of people sharing that cluster are visible, body language and facial expression offer all sorts of nonverbal and visual cues about when it makes sense to interrupt. Software developers can tell by looking at another screen what someone is working on, without asking. They can also judge easily and instantaneously, by observing body language, whether someone is totally engrossed or open to conversation. These nonverbal cues reduce unwanted interruption. The close proximity and visual access make spontaneous communication and interaction easy. The outcome is tacit learning, learning on the job, just in time, informally from those you observe and overhear around you. These layouts redefine what needs to be private, as happens in a close-knit family. By taking an "activity-based" approach to workplace design, as we'll see later in this chapter, companies can create separate, closed rooms to which people retreat as needed.

The small scale of this team-oriented cluster makes informal communication easy, helps people get to know each other, and contributes to team identity.

For many employees, the preferred solution to the problem of managing unwanted interruptions is the closed office. It can do that, but it does so at the expense of facilitating the social relationships and information flow that are the hallmark of effective knowledge networks. Yet if you survey employees in a closed office whether they communicate frequently with colleagues, they invariably say they do. But employee surveys assessing the effect of differing office types on communication patterns by themselves can paint a misleading picture. Our own studies at Cornell, for example, showed virtually no differences in the amount of communication reported by engineers working in closed offices compared to cubes and team-oriented bullpens. Everyone felt they communicated a lot. Our ethnographic data, based on in-depth interviews, told a very different story.[13]

The Price of Privacy

In a closed office communication was highly controlled ("We definitely schedule meetings. We rarely have ad hoc meetings here. Usually we'll pick some times to meet."). People in a closed office viewed conference calls, e-mail, and scheduled meetings as permitting sufficient communication. Most said it was a more productive work environment than a cubicle, since they could control the pace of their work and perhaps even achieve in an hour, day, or week what they set out to do. Furthermore, the closed office can reinforce authority, as much by what it keeps out as what it lets in. Occupants were less likely to overhear others' personal conversations (and freer to engage in their own) and were less likely to see others nodding off to sleep, snacking at their desk, or shopping on eBay. This insulation helps preserve a sense of decorum and dignity easily lost when everyday behavior of this sort is made visible. In short, not having to interact with others serendipitously and being able to structure one's own work to maximize personal productivity were seen as a distinct benefit.

Yet some of those in closed offices recognized that their privacy carried a price. Physical separation reduced communication with colleagues, which weakened the project or team's performance even though it might not affect (or might even improve) their own individual performance. As one software engineer noted: "We suffer because we don't have much of a sense of team. And I don't think people understand the relationship of their work to others . . . Because they don't have this fabric of a team, they don't understand when they're not performing well that they're impacting somebody else."[14]

Coping with Cubes

In a conventional closed office, we all have learned what constitutes civilized behavior. People knock before entering. If we don't want to be disturbed, we close the door. The problem with most open office environments, particularly cubicles, is that we're unsure what constitutes civilized behavior. What do you do when you overhear a telephone conversation and you realize you have information that could help resolve a problem, but you don't want to admit that you overheard the conversation? As a network engineer commented, "When we were in cubicles we still sat very close to each other and I would overhear bits and pieces . . . and it felt invasive. I felt like I was stepping on a conversation that I wasn't invited into. And my choice was I could either be obnoxious or I could sit there and pretend I didn't hear it."[15]

In an environment without doors, we constantly say hello to people as they pass by or poke a head into our workstation. Not engaging in such everyday social intercourse takes considerable energy, since it goes against the grain of what we have come to think of as civilized behavior. If we don't do it, we feel guilty and anxious. We worry that others will consider us impolite or snooty, even though all we are trying to do is get our work done.

Over the course of a day, these ten-, twenty-, and thirty-second chats generate a lot of interaction, but not much productive interchange. The panel might afford visual privacy, but we can still hear our cube neighbors chat or fight on the phone with a girlfriend, talk with the doctor, or describe in excruciating detail the benefits of the latest investment program about which we could care less. Worse, almost all of this kind of interaction is uncontrollable. Research by my colleague Gary Evans and others has shown that perceived control, the sense that you can control unwanted interruptions or sounds, is the key factor in mediating people's response to noise (or in fact determining what is noise and what is not).[16]

All sorts of attempts have been made to deal with noise in the cubicle environment, none of them very successfully.

The problem isn't purely technical, nor is the solution. To address these social and cultural glitches, a logical step is to create "office protocols" that specify the kinds of behavior that can mitigate the negative aspects of living in an open plan environment. Protocols can actually help if done right, since they do sensitize people to and make discussible behavior that offends or annoys others, often unintentionally (see Chapter Nine, "Managing Workspace Change").

Still, employees in cubicles complain about noise. The first solution most people consider when trying to figure out how to reduce the problem of noise in a panel-based workstation is raising the height of the panels, and covering the panels with fabric and other materials designed to absorb sound rather than reflect it. Unfortunately, as Alan Hedge, another Cornell colleague and leading human factors and ergonomics expert, points out, neither solution really solves the problem since sound tends to go up and then bounce down from the ceiling, not just flow horizontally from mouth to ear.

For many firms, the next line of defense in fighting the noise associated with open plan cubicles is fighting noise with noise. "White" noise or sound-masking systems push air through heating ducts to create a constant but indistinct sound intended not to eliminate human conversation but to make it uninterpretable. Human factor specialists refer to this as reducing "speech intelligibility." We can hear people talking but cannot understand what they are saying. Since we are more likely to pay attention to content than just the sound of speech, to human factor specialists rendering speech unintelligible is an efficient way of reducing problems with noise. We experience the concept all the time in a crowded and noisy café. There, no single voice stands out, commanding our attention. However, the problem in still other offices is not that they are too noisy but that they are too quiet. In a room where you can hear a pin drop, the voice of an enthusiastic sales rep on the phone rings out like a siren in the night.

In the end, employees assess a workplace in terms of how it feels to work in it and whether they believe it allows them to work productively, not whether it increases space efficiency and reduces real estate costs—or even whether scientific data show that the sound level should be acceptable. Research by Michael Brill and his associates[17] as well as our own studies show that despite all the furniture, technical, and social fixes that have been tried to render cubicles more acceptable to employees, on the whole cubicles flunk.

Managing Scale

The debate about open versus closed offices and how they influence communication patterns and social and knowledge networks as well as the ability to concentrate and work without disruption typically is framed around the issue of openness (and lack of privacy). But the fundamental problem with panel-based open plan systems has less to do with openness than it does with the *scale* of the open plan environment found in many a large organization. Open plan offices as we have come to know them through the last third of the twentieth century are gigantic. In comparison to the smaller-scale shared offices common around the turn of the century and earlier, and still found in Scandinavian and European offices, many open plan office floors today flow like the Nile at flood tide over as much as forty thousand square feet. Were such a floor a lake, we would do better navigating it with motor rather than oar. These are alienating social spaces, despite their putative focus on facilitating communication. Office planners may describe a vast plain of workstations with the language of a city, complete with neighborhoods and communities, cafés and streets, but they feel more like a barren landscape, mind-numbing not in its emptiness, but in its vast size and uniformity.

Small, team-oriented clusters create an entirely different social dynamic from a room the size of an Indiana cornfield filled with cubicles. In the former, one develops personal relationships with neighbors. As in any community, some of the relationships are smoother, friendlier, and more comfortable than others. But a smaller social setting can enhance work processes. In a room with five to ten others, or in an area within a floor occupied by twenty-five to fifty people, we quickly learn more about our coworkers than their technical prowess or knowledge. We come to know their strengths and weaknesses, workstyle, reliability, and trustworthiness. Is this someone with whom I can share my knowledge and still trust that she will give me due credit? Will she reciprocate with support and information when I need it? Who is effective under pressure? Who really knows how this organization works and what it takes (and whom one needs to know) to get things done? We don't have to search a massive database to find out who we might contact for information we need immediately. We ask around in our group, and the powers of the network quickly identify the right person to contact.

The importance of scale cannot be overestimated. The good news is that with some imagination a large space can be subdivided into smaller ones at minimal cost and great effectiveness. Furniture maker Herman Miller did this in renovating a factory space for its own headquarters in Zeeland, Michigan. Using what they called "fat walls," thick panels that snaked around the building, the people at Herman Miller created a sense of a street with neighborhoods radiating off it. The smaller areas, defined by the thick walls, created more intimate spaces in the huge, hangarlike manufacturing space. *An open environment doesn't have to be bought at the expense of small scale.*

Balancing Individual and Team Performance

The value of a knowledge network is clear if individual productivity and team effectiveness are viewed as flip sides of the same coin. Teams, even more so than individuals, depend on the free flow of information: sharing ideas, expertise, and specific techniques; providing timely feedback; developing consensus about goals and objectives; identifying best practices and making sure everyone learns about them quickly; helping others solve problems. All of this in turn depends on getting to know others well enough to trust their judgment, their discretion, their fairness, their expertise.

Small groupings of people working closely together make that possible. As a Web designer commented, "Being able to establish social relationships definitely helps me work better. I feel like it's much less of an imposition to ask questions and I can save time. And I feel more comfortable asking for help or getting input."[18]

This isn't to say that small team environments don't create tension. They do. We can learn more than we wish about our colleagues. We don't like everyone with whom we work. But despite the most sophisticated advances in the technology of communication, from e-mail and mobile phones to instant messaging and desk-based videoconferencing, we still depend on and prefer face-to-face communication for interaction requiring subtle messages, whether it takes the form of brainstorming or performance feedback. Small-scale, team-oriented clusters foster unsurpassed opportunities for this kind of interaction. Unlike the traditional assembly line or the complete craft-oriented teams found until recently in firms such as Volvo, these small-scale team environments do not presuppose that employees should or can always be on task, or that chatting and socializing necessarily constitutes nonwork.

Zoning

Careful zoning of activities and functions, in conjunction with the principle of small-scale clusters, helps mitigate the noise of unwanted conversation in an open team-oriented environment. Locating a software developer or lawyer within overhearing distance of a marketing person is like locating elderly housing next to a teen center because you believe both can benefit from the other's experience. Nice theory. Engineers and lawyers work on different problems, using different tools, with different work styles. Dogs and cats sometimes get along, but it is not a good idea to depend on it.

Affinity zoning—locating software developers near software developers, for example, or human resource people near human resource people—makes better sense. Ironically, cross-functional teaming violates this more common practice—that is, mixing engineers and marketing people together, for example, so both understand each other better. One solution is to mix clusters of different disciplines together, so that three or four engineers sit together but in a team along with three or four marketing people. This is an opportunity for conversation around one's expertise, as well as to interact more often and easily with others your work affects.

When Alcoa was planning its new headquarters, for example, the goal was to integrate purchasing people and tax lawyers because useful tax advice was needed early on in structuring deals and negotiations, not after the fact. Co-location was viewed as a way for each discipline to better understand what the other was doing, and how they could both be useful to each other. The legal staff, in particular, were not enthusiastic, especially if someone might be the only lawyer in a cross-functional group. In this case the company dedicated some space in another group's area, with the understanding that the lawyer (or human resource or finance expert) would spend a part of every week working in this area while maintaining an assigned space within her own department. This approach recognizes the value of working regularly with others in their own space rather than just meeting for an hour or two periodically in a conference room. But it does so without sacrificing the benefits of working with colleagues in one's own discipline.

Another alternative is functional zoning that groups specific kinds of tasks, regardless of who is doing them, together. In KPMG Peat Marwick's offices in Stockholm, consultants who come into the office for a short period of time used a "touchdown" section of a floor, comprising small worksurfaces that slide up and down on a pole (so that they can be used sitting or standing by someone of any height) to check their e-mail, chat, and catch up with others doing the same thing. If they wanted to concentrate while writing a report or analyzing data, they moved to another part of the same floor separated from the touchdown area by seven-foot-high screens. Here, there were more con-

A quiet place to concentrate can be achieved without high walls by zoning activities in a defined area and combining this with "protocols" about not talking or using telephones in the quiet zone.

ventional workstations, but without panels separating them from each other. Auditory privacy was obtained by the people working on that floor agreeing that when you worked in the quiet zone you would not use a phone or talk with other people.

The Future of the Closed Office

Given the pivotal role of information flow and knowledge networks in today's organizations, what role does the closed office play? In the face of corporate America's vaunted commitment to productivity, one might expect the allure of the closed office to have faded long ago. I've seen little convincing evidence that people working in a private, single-occupant closed office are more productive than their counterparts working in an open office. Indeed, in one of the few recent studies with hard performance data (based on actual output rather than self-reported measures of performance), University of Michigan researchers on software development teams found that productivity, in terms of both quantity and quality of code written, was almost twice as high for teams working in a shared "war room" compared to individual workstations. This was attributed to an enhanced level of free-flowing communication and interaction between the programmers in the team space.[19]

Reconciling Competing Needs

The reality is that small-scale, team-oriented, open plan clusters designed as part of an activity-based workplace strategy have myriad benefits. More expensive, less flexible closed offices undermine interaction and render tacit learning nearly impossible. Yet the vast majority of people, in just about any job and at any level, prefer having their own fully enclosed office. Finding the right balance between satisfying employee preferences and work patterns that benefit the team and organization (not just the individual) is truly a wicked problem; it has no easy answers.

Acknowledging Rank

The amount of space we're assigned and its quality of view, materials, and furniture is an environmental message that tells us and others about our standing in the team, department, or enterprise as a whole. Others' perceptions of us, including friends, family, and professional colleagues, are shaped in part by where we work and the kind of offices we inhabit. These views, in turn, influence our own personal and professional identity. The deep emotional currents and passionate debates stimulated by decisions about who will get a closed office or the office with the best view or the newest furniture put the lie to the argument that space isn't that important. Normally mild-mannered, fairly reasonable men and women go ballistic, descend into depression, and fight like pit bulls when they find they've been moved from a small (even if grungy) office to a workstation, which could be sparkling new.

Peter Miscovich, a partner in PriceWaterhouseCoopers' Advisory Services, explains this deep emotional response as a fight for "authentication." We want to be recognized for our achievements and standing in the firm. We fight for a closed office on the grounds of utility but covet it emotionally. We say "I need an office to be able to concentrate" or "I don't care about an office, but my clients expect me to have one and won't take me seriously if I don't have one" or "We are required to keep this kind of information confidential from those working with other clients." Few people are prepared to stand up and fight for a closed office on the basis that they are entitled to one because of their rank and status within the company ("Hey, I'm an important guy!"). This is not the case in off-record comments. In conversations of this kind people willingly talk about feeling entitled to an office because of their position as a vice president or senior manager ("Dammit, I've worked here for fifteen years, and I expect to get an office when I'm promoted").

American workers publicly justify a closed office in terms of its utility because, even though they want to be recognized for their contributions, they are ambivalent about *privilege* and the perquisites of rank and status that follow from it. Other cultures are less confused and embarrassed by clear expression of privilege. In Germany and much of Latin America, a large and sumptuous office, or simply an office in any form, is recognized and accepted as a legitimate perquisite of rank. Managers don't justify office size or the quality of furniture in terms of their performance enhancement. In America, our populist beliefs and democratic values lead us to shade status distinctions. We blur and mask them under the rhetoric of performance and utility rather than entitlement or authentication.

We don't need to, and should not pretend, that such status distinctions do not exist or matter to people. They do. But we might want to consider ways of dealing with status and privilege other than by reflexive resort to offices that increase costs, reduce flexibility, and restrict the flow of information.

Giving people a closed office isn't the only way to recognize their standing in the firm. The military denotes status with ribbons and stars. They are inexpensive, portable, visible, and understood by everyone. Is it ludicrous to think that a firm might develop fashion accessories like lapel pins, scarves, and ties to convey rank and status? This purely symbolic messaging is the purpose served by the colored bits of carpet outside offices in the U.S. Treasury Department in Washington, D.C. Awarding high performers with more exciting projects, more responsibility, the opportunity to choose one's staff and team members, as well as promotions, salary, bonus, and stock options recognizes status without relying on space, one of the organization's most expensive resources apart from the employees themselves.

For impressing clients, a sumptuous conference room rather than a private office can convey the financial success, good taste, and stability of the firm. Years ago IBM took this approach in their 590 Madison sales headquarters in the heart of Manhattan. All the executives shared—long before the word *hoteling* entered the lexicon of office designing—four offices on the top floor of the building, with magnificent views and furnished in impeccable executive taste. When executives were in residence, they met clients in whichever of these offices were available, or in equally well-appointed meeting rooms. Japanese executives follow the same pattern. Their day-to-day office is a plain desk, perhaps slightly larger than the standard desk, which looks out on staff working at the armada of desks on the floor. When VIP visitors arrive, the executive repairs to his ceremonial office for tea and polite conversation. Status is here to stay. Why not recognize it in a way that uses the corporation's scarce resources to the fullest potential?

Activity-Based Planning

No single office solution is perfect. All involve trade-offs. The cubicle is efficient in terms of its space requirements but not especially conducive to communication, concentration, or even flexibility. The closed office makes concentration and private conversation easier, but it is expensive and inflexible and impedes spontaneous, free-form communication. The team-oriented cluster is efficient and flexible; it enhances the sense of community and communication but affords no opportunity for psychological retreat. One solution is to begin to think of the office not as the place within the building where the individual works most of the time but as a series of loosely coupled settings both inside and outside the office connected by the electronic movement of information and the physical movement of people. When Alcoa sold its old landmark tower in the center of Pittsburgh and moved across the river to a new low-rise building, every corner was designed for work, from one's workstation to the cafeteria. To capture the idea that one could work anywhere in the building, Marty Powell, the building's architect, described the basic office size as three hundred thousand square feet—the size of the whole building, not the individual workstation.

The physical manifestation of this concept is what has become known as activity-based planning. Rather than assuming an individual will do all his work while in the office building in one place, and then trying to design that place to support every conceivable work activity (telephoning, writing, reading, thinking, meetings, analyzing), the concept is to create a series of work settings. Each is designed to support a particular kind of activity especially well. This extends the logic of zoning in a more far-reaching design strategy. Mobility within the office becomes the norm. Over the course of the day you select from the range of available work settings those that make the most sense for you, depending on the kind of work you are doing.

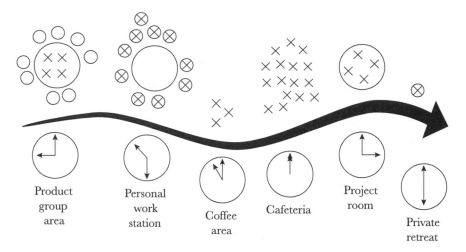

Product group area

Personal work station

Coffee area

Cafeteria

Project room

Private retreat

Figure 2.1. A variety of settings for a variety of tasks. In an activity-based workspace strategy, individuals choose where to work over the course of a day or week according to their preferred workstyle, the nature of the work, and the needs of team members.

For an informal conversation you might meet in the coffee lounge and sit on high stools at a small round bar or table such as you might find in a bar or café. For a confidential conversation or to read a report, you might use the cafeteria during its off hours or find a couple of easy chairs tucked into a corner. When clients arrive for a presentation, you meet them in a well-appointed conference room with state-of-the-art media technology. When you want to read an article or surf the Web, the library makes sense. Need to push out a report on deadline? Book a small, fully enclosed room without telephone but with a computer or network access for your laptop, where you can concentrate without interruption. No longer is the choice between open or closed. It is both open and closed, formal and informal, individual and team. The *basic* kit for an activity-based work system includes space, technology, and management practices working in harmony. However, this approach also requires management commitment to mobility and diversity of workstyles, for both individuals and entire departments. Activity-based planning will fail if (1) the company doesn't create truly diverse and distinct spaces and (2) managers don't encourage staff to choose to use these varied settings to work wherever they can be most productive for that particular task, inside or outside the office.

Ultimately, space is not about real estate. It is about using all of the organization's scarce resources to meet pressing business challenges. In today's global marketplace, companies that have the best chance not just to survive but thrive are the ones that most effectively develop and exploit knowledge. Doing so means recognizing that the office as we have known it over the past fifty to one hundred years is an idea shaped by values, technology, and design that largely ignored how and where knowledge networks are formed, and how they can best be exploited to gain competitive market advantage. The office was once a more social space, and as we launch the twenty-first century it has become that again.

Implications for Practice

- Create small-scale, truly open environments, where people can see each other and read nonverbal cues without standing up or walking through a door or around a panel.
- Have a range of places to meet, some permitting full privacy, so a meeting can occur that contains the noise of loud voices, laughter, or rowdy debate. Vary room size and transparency. Not every meeting area or conference room has to be glass-fronted, but some should be.
- Vary the level of physical informality. Bar-height stools and tables, or cafeteria-style tables, foster an informal setting for conversation that differs considerably in tone and message from sofas and easy chairs. Blurring the distinction between work and nonwork reduces the risk of being seen in public just "relaxing" by a manager or coworker who may be unsure of whether "real" work happens outside one's work-station, office, or laboratory.
- Provide panel and wall space throughout the office where people can post works in progress—diagrams and drawings, flow charts, lists of goals, or summaries of accomplishments. If the group or unit creates products that are physical devices or equipment, make a space where they can be seen by others not directly working on them. (Sensitive materials can be displayed in an area off limits to outside visitors—or the company's own employees if there is a demonstrably good reason for doing so.)
- Create a culture where high disclosure is valued, not feared. There isn't any point in offering wallspace for displayed thinking that would be punished if used!
- Think of a range of routine activities as potential "activity generators." Strategically grouping toilets, coffee and beverage areas, copy machines, and even a TV (for news, stock reports, and so on) together acts as a natural magnet for people.
- Carefully locate circulation paths so that they maximize the potential for unplanned, "opportunistic" meetings. Circulation that draws people by and through magnet activity zones increases the potential for people meeting one another.
- Think of circulation as less like a highway, where fast and efficient throughput of people is the goal, and more like a country lane, where leisurely wandering with occasional stops for a chat with a neighbor or popping into a small shop is the

pattern. Encourage people who might accidentally run into each other to stop and chat, by using design features such as wide wooden railings comfortably angled to support someone leaning on them while talking with a friend. Wider corridors, or standard corridors with meeting or seating or chatting spaces breaking up the corridor every once in a while, increase the visibility and eye contact that trigger conversation.

- Hang photographs of employees with brief descriptions of what they work on or their area of expertise along circulation routes near where people sit, so that passers-by get a sense of what is going on in that group or unit without having to ask or make a concerted effort to find out. Pique interest without making a big fuss about it.
- Combine planned events with informal meeting opportunities. At Oxford University almost every lecture or seminar is followed by drinks, a kind of intellectually stimulated cocktail party. It's not unlike having to go on the winery tour to partake of the wine tasting.

CHAPTER THREE

CO-LOCATION

Bringing everyone under one roof helps communication and collaboration,
if the roof isn't very large.

As companies evolve they outgrow floors, and then buildings and even campuses. Face-to-face daily interaction across teams, departments, and the organization as a whole breaks down. We rely instead on twenty-first-century drums and smoke signals: the telephone and e-mail vaporize distance, whether we're working with people in the next building or ten thousand miles away. But for most of us, and for most organizations, co-location—being in the same office—is still preferred. The richness of information, verbal and nonverbal, that can be shared is without peer. We like getting to know other people and use that knowledge to build the trust that unlocks our willingness to share the information, insights, knowledge, and experience on which productive work and effective organizations depend.

How Close Is Close Enough?

Our sense that proximity helps us communicate effectively is well founded. Yet co-locating thousands of employees on a single campus or in one large building in hopes of enhancing face-to-face communication often produces disappointing results.

Research shows that proximity matters a great deal. But it only does so in very close proximity. In studies of dozens of engineering design teams in the United States and Britain over a twenty-five-year period, MIT Professor Thomas Allen consistently found that face-to-face interaction declined dramatically beyond about fifty meters.[1]

Organizational reporting relationships extend the distance at which face-to-face interaction occurs, but only slightly. Even with strong organizational connections, the frequency of face-to-face interaction declined markedly in less than the length of half a football field.

The same pattern holds for research scientists. Robert Kraut and his associates at Bell Labs studied the influence of physical proximity on the collaborative relationships between scientific researchers in industry.[2] Pairs of researchers on the same floor as each other were about six times more likely to enter into research collaboration than pairs on different floors or in different buildings. Beyond this short span, however, increasing distance doesn't seem to make much difference in the amount of contact. Robert Sommer, chair of the University of California, Davis, psychology department, and his students discovered this more than a decade ago when they looked at communication and collaboration patterns across research centers on the Davis campus.[3] Longer physical distance didn't significantly reduce the amount of reported contact across the centers and institutes. Far more important was the perceived value of the potential contact. When perceived as valuable, more contact occurred; when not, then contact was low regardless of distance. Proximity by itself, unless it is within a very short distance, is unlikely to lead to a significant level of personal contact.

What's the Value of a Corporate Campus?

Most of the available research on communication and co-location, like that just described, concerns dedicated project teams—groups working together on a specific task over a given period of time. Much less is known about the value of co-location for business units such as a department or division which have weaker relationships than dedicated teams yet could benefit from greater understanding and stronger collaboration. At this larger organizational scale, companies also face critical co-location decisions. Will consolidating employees in numerous departments and divisions around fifteen leased buildings into a single corporate tower or corporate campus actually translate into more frequent and effective face-to-face communication and collaboration?

We explored this issue as part of our Cornell International Workplace Studies Program (IWSP) research.[4] Using a Web-based survey, we've collected data from more than four thousand employees at four sites. One was an urban campus created by the purchase and leasing over time of several buildings within a five-block area within New York City's financial district. The second was a suburban campus comprising both owned and leased buildings acquired over time, but with no single architectural style or character. The third and fourth were prototypical corporate campuses, purpose-built in a greenfield location with a consistent and distinctive architectural style.

Diminishing Returns for Campuses

Overall, the results for people in finance, marketing, corporate real estate, and other corporate headquarters functions mirror those for teams of research scientists and engineers. The frequency of interaction dropped off significantly as distance increased both *organizationally* (from one's own team to one's own department, another department, and then another division); and *physically* (expanding the scale of one's own floor, own building, or other building) across all sites. More than 90 percent of the respondents met at least once a week with someone from their own group or team, compared with about 50 percent meeting at least once a week with someone from another division. The percentage meeting more than once a week was negligible. The findings for the effects of physical location followed a similar pattern. These meetings may be useful, but given that a significant percentage of respondents said a combination of e-mail and telephone (including teleconferences) worked effectively for these occasional nondepartmental meetings, co-location on a large scale may not be worth the cost and effort.

The general pattern was clear: interaction declined dramatically beyond *one's own floor and one's own workgroup*. After that point, there is little further decline in face-to-face interaction as distance increases, whether a few hundred yards or several miles. The exception occurs when there is a strong functional relationship between physically separated groups several miles apart. In the company we studied where this occurred, a high level of interaction occurred in a building fifteen minutes away by car (about ten miles) because of its strong functional connection to the headquarters building on the main campus. Less interaction occurred in physically closer buildings, including those right next to each other, that lacked a strong functional relationship.

Scheduled Versus Unscheduled Meetings

In terms of personal interaction, one of the presumed benefits of co-location on a campus is that there are more unscheduled face-to-face meetings than when meetings require getting on a plane or into a car, or taking the company's shuttle bus. Yet even when no transport was required, unscheduled meetings occurred with some frequency only within one's own group or team (neighbors on the same floor), and only when involving one other person.

We were also curious about how much in advance scheduled meetings are arranged. Theoretically, meetings on a compact, purpose-built campus, even though scheduled, might be arranged on shorter notice because it takes minimum time and effort to meet anywhere on the campus. Again, the results didn't bear this out. On the most compact campus, 50 percent of meetings were scheduled two to five days in advance, and 39 percent more than one week in advance. Given that lead time, traveling to a meeting within, say, a fifty-mile radius is not terribly difficult.

Productive Versus Wasted Time

The argument against dispersed offices, of course, is that all the travel time is wasted. Organizations thinking along these lines typically demonstrate their point by doing a time and travel study. The total number of trips multiplied by the average length of each trip is multiplied by an average salary. The results are predictable: millions of dollars are being spent on travel to and from buildings. But does a big number always justify a change? GE Aircraft Engines, which occupies an enormous campus complex outside Cincinnati, Ohio, had over the years acquired a number of leased offices within about a ten-mile radius of the main campus. They were trying to determine whether it was worthwhile to bring all these people back onto the main campus, so they did a time and travel study. When I first saw the results, which showed that about $4 million dollars was spent in travel time annually, I thought it was pretty obvious that a significant amount of money was being wasted. Management was unimpressed. They thought not in terms of M's (millions of dollars) but in terms of B's (billions of dollars). For GE Aircraft Engines, $4 million was a drop in the bucket. Given the cost and disruption of bringing people back to the main campus, the potential savings was not a particularly convincing rationale.

Another way of determining whether time spent traveling between buildings is wasted takes a different tack: it tries to understand how employees use the journey time. Does the time spent walking between floors or across a campus, or driving to a site a few miles away, have any value? When we asked employees how they used their journey time, 60 percent reported walking to a meeting with someone else at least once a week. While walking together, almost 95 percent of the respondents talked about work-related matters: getting ready for a meeting, talking about other business, debriefing, and planning the next steps after a meeting. The social conversations that occurred regularly on the journey to meetings were interspersed with work-related conversations and were valued for helping build personal relationships. These conversations in turn helped smooth work relationships. Even when traveling alone to a meeting, almost everyone interviewed felt the time was productive; they used the time to make phone calls or to check and return voice and e-mails. The only situation in which travel time seemed a waste was when the amount of time needed to reach their destination was uncertain, a common complaint when using public transportation such as trains and ferries.

Value of Meetings

Employees distinguish between two kinds of meeting: those that are regularly scheduled for the purpose of checking the status of a project and to coordinate efforts, and project meetings focused on solving specific problems. The latter require dialogue and group work and are highly valued. By contrast, employees need little excuse to miss a status meeting. We found people calling in to meetings rather than attending in person, despite being only a few doors down the hall. That way they could look like good citizens, even as they put the phone on mute and carried on an unrelated conversation in their office, checked e-mail, or read a report. People highly valued co-location and face-to-face communication with their *own team or group*, if the meeting was about solving problems. For just about everything and everyone else, they were confident in electronic communication as a means of keeping in touch, monitoring progress, and other fairly routine activities.

Corporate Identity and Commitment

From an organizational perspective, increased interaction isn't the only possible benefit of co-location on a corporate campus. Companies want their employees to identify with the company because stronger identification generally translates into greater commitment. This in turn is associated with giving more of oneself in terms of energy and ideas. We know that professional employees identify most with their own team or project and their profession. The company as a whole is further down the list (sometimes below one's customers). Particularly for more mobile employees, companies worry that spending time away from the campus may undermine a strong sense of corporate identification. Given that companies spend millions of dollars on facilities, the question of whether and how the planning and design of these contribute first to attraction and retention and second to identification is far from trivial.

The corporate campuses we've studied differed markedly in their design, as noted earlier. Some were purpose-built and architecturally distinct; others were more a group of buildings in relatively close proximity without any consistent architectural image. The working assumption for many campus advocates is that a strong, branded campus conveys power, prestige, and stability to prospective employees. The company isn't likely to disappear, the thinking goes, if it can afford a corporate campus. This sense of being part of a significant enterprise contributes, many practitioners believe, to attraction and retention. Again, our research suggests otherwise. The critical factor in someone's decision to join or remain with a firm was the nature of the job and compensation, followed by the location of the campus within the United States. Also important, but less so than compensation and the job itself, were the people one works with, one's immediate manager, and pride in working for a major company. What employees cared about most in terms of physical factors was the distance of the campus from their home. A short commute time was highly valued. Anyone who has experienced a corporate move can recite war stories demonstrating just how emotional people can become about what may appear to project planners as a relatively slight dislocation.

What differences we found in employees' sense of belonging were not related to how architecturally distinct the campuses were. The most distinctive campus architecturally, at least in our small sample, did not have employees reporting the highest level of corporate identity. Employees noticed and paid attention to the image of their company conveyed through its physical design. However, a stronger factor in employees' identification with the company than the building's exterior architectural style and form was the interior design and layout. These findings suggest that strong employee identification can be achieved without necessarily having strong, architecturally branded (and possibly more expensive) campus buildings. An added benefit of paying more attention to interior design and worrying less about exterior image and architectural style is that it may be easier, should the need arise, to sublet or sell a portion of an architecturally unbranded campus than one with a strong, single, corporate image that prospective tenants feel might overshadow their own identity.

Principles for Workplace Planning

Our research suggests that co-locating buildings on a corporate campus is unlikely to result in a relatively high level of face-to-face interaction beyond one's own group or team, or beyond one's own floor, whether in planned or unplanned meetings. From a co-location perspective, this means that if face-to-face interaction is valued, the single important facility decision is who goes on the same floor. Beyond that, face-to-face interaction drops off so dramatically that it may not make a great deal of difference which groups are located on which floors or in which buildings. Efforts to restack multistory buildings or to relocate whole groups from one building to another in the expectation that being under one roof will significantly increase personal interaction, collaboration, and mutual understanding may not be worth doing, given the cost and disruption involved.

It may, however, be worthwhile to relocate a whole department so that the entire department is co-located on the same floor. This is likely not only to increase interaction within a department but also to lead to a stronger sense of belonging with the company. This might mean, for example, that it makes more sense for a large department that expands beyond the capacity of another floor to move as a whole unit to another building rather than hiving off that part of the department that no longer can be accommodated on a single floor. Alternatively, if the department is split, who goes and who stays should be determined with a clear understanding of which parts of the department would benefit most from being in close proximity. The unit that does end up off the main department floor could, from this perspective, be moved not to just the next closest space (for instance, an adjacent floor or building) but to the space that generates the least amount of cost or disruption to *other* groups, even if this means being several floors or a building away.

It may also make more sense, when a whole department can no longer fit on a single floor, to split the department into two or more large blocks, rather than to retain most of the department on one floor but place a much smaller contingent in another location. Two larger contingents are more likely to create a sense of being part of the whole department than being a very small group co-located with a different department. In all cases, the key question is, Who will benefit most from being co-located on the same floor? The key lesson is that in terms of the likelihood of face-to-face interaction, being in close proximity means on the same floor, not in the same building or on a campus.

The underlying question is not whether people prefer face-to-face meetings. Most of the time, they do. It is whether co-location on a corporate campus or tower is critical, or only the ability to get to a meeting within a relatively short distance or travel time. Given the comparative infrequency of face-to-face meetings beyond one's own department and own floor, the fact that most such meetings are scheduled in advance, and that a high percentage of employees believe e-mail is effective for communicating with most people beyond the work group, co-location may not be critical to enhancing collaboration across the enterprise.

This isn't to say that employees don't appreciate amenities such as cafeterias and fitness centers made possible by the economies of scale of a corporate campus. However, it is not clear that employees faced with a choice between a full-service cafeteria or fitness center and a significantly shortened commute would prefer the amenities and the campus whose scale justifies them. In assessing the value of co-location and a corporate campus, many factors interact in complex ways that preclude simple cause-and-effect explanation.

Particularly intriguing are buildings both too close and too far from the main campus. Two of the companies we studied had a main campus and some ancillary buildings within a distance of ten to twenty miles. Interview data at both sites suggested that those off the main campus still felt its gravitational pull, while being sufficiently outside the orbit to be able to exploit all its amenities and opportunities. They felt neither part of the main campus nor remote enough to establish their own corporate identity. As a result, those off the main campus felt like second-class citizens despite all the best efforts of the corporation to provide campuslike amenities.

The Organizational Ecology Perspective

As noted in the Introduction, the central tenet of organizational ecology is that no single element of a workplace strategy outweighs all others. Increased interaction and collaboration is rarely the only reason a company chooses to co-locate employees. Even when this is a major factor for co-location, the building can never force interaction by itself. Like water flowing downhill, a well-designed building can make interaction easier or more difficult, requiring more or less employee effort. Centralized common areas such as a corporate cafeteria and fitness center create opportunities for people from various business units to interact. But a large number of employees don't necessarily use such facilities, and even when they do they are more likely to interact with people they already know.

Overcoming distance between floors or across buildings necessarily involves design of social systems as well as interior and building design. These social systems range from promoting communities of nonwork interest, such as social clubs that bring together people from a number of departments and divisions with a shared passion for cooking, movies, or hiking, to more direct social engineering. This takes the form of deliberately co-locating individuals and teams from departments and divisions who organizational leaders believe would directly benefit from closer working relationships on the same floor, and preferably being close together on that floor. At this point, micro design features such as common meeting and break areas can act as activity magnets, drawing people together, but from a close distance. Just bringing everyone together under one roof is unlikely by itself (as this chapter underscores) to drive increased collaboration across business units. It is the particular combination and interplay of social and environmental factors that determines whether the co-location workspace strategy works.

Implications for Practice

- *Be clear about strategic goals and objectives.* If the goal is to plant a flag in a new location, as Sun Microsystems did when they built their campus outside Denver, to demonstrate to prospective employees and the surrounding community a commitment to an area, then a corporate campus can make sense. A corporate campus can also make sense if opportunities for expansion within the campus are matched by an exit strategy, whether sale or lease, that minimizes the likelihood of owning more space than needed in a weak or fast-changing market. With goals of this kind, limited cross-unit interaction isn't a major drawback. It would be if that were a primary rationale for pursuing a campus strategy

- *Test and challenge common working assumptions.* The fundamental question is the conditions under which having everyone under one roof as part of a large scale co-location actually (1) reduces facility and technology and operational costs and (2) increases long-term flexibility (including growth and exit opportunities), staff attraction and retention, teamwork and collaboration, branding and image, and business continuity.

- *Locate or remain in a desirable national location.* Simply stated, people want to work in nice places. The critical factor is that a sufficiently large and appropriate employee population exist in regions or cities employees consider desirable. Staying in the same location within a region is not necessary for daily interaction purposes, but being within a thirty- to sixty-minute travel time can be useful for meetings that are likely to occur twice or three times a week. Beyond that, distance is not likely to be an important factor.
- *Develop distributed building nodes.* Employees greatly value being able to work near where they live. The key benefits of a campus for employees, particularly dining and fitness facilities, are unlikely to outweigh the benefit of a shorter commute. A number of building nodes strategically placed to reflect residential patterns can reduce commute time without undermining important interaction within departments and work teams.
- *Balance different benefits.* Working across many locations underscores a series of trade-offs. Given the right conditions, the benefits of distributed departments and divisions are likely to outweigh the loss of short and easy travel to occasional meetings with those outside one's own group or team.
- *Co-locate highly interdependent groups within a building.* The most critical decision is which groups and departments to locate on the same floor. Locating departments and divisions on a campus with several buildings spread out over dozens or more acres is likely to have little effect on interaction across departments and divisions.
- *Avoid major and minor nodes.* Concern about creating second-class citizens is justified. The sense of missing out and being given poorer quality amenities is more likely to occur when an off-campus building is located within about a ten- to twenty-mile radius of a main campus than when the building is far enough away to become its own node.
- *Consider specialized nodes.* A node may have special emphasis (a trading node, laboratory node, marketing node), but the specialized facilities are in this case directly related to function, not to standing within the company. An R&D node that furnishes laboratory space for several departments more efficiently uses the highly specialized and expensive infrastructure needed.
- *Brand for employees with interior layout and design.* Employees value the nature of their own office or workstation more than the overall layout and design of a floor or campus, or a campus itself. One value of a distributed office node is that it may be possible to increase the amount of office space at a cost comparable to providing less space in more expensive real estate in a central area. When combined with shorter commute time, this is likely to be an attractive workplace strategy for employees.
- *Build technical infrastructure.* Build the technological infrastructure to allow anyone to communicate with anyone else in the organization, wherever they may be

located, including from home or other noncompany sites. The basic requirement is compatible equipment and high-speed networks, laptop computers, intranets, and easy and fast connection protocols that make e-mail and sending and receiving large documents fast and easy.

- *Provide some fitness and dining within the building(s).* The two amenities employees valued most were fitness and dining. These can be made available in a relatively small corporate node, albeit on a less grand scale than on a major campus.

CHAPTER FOUR

THE RIGHT SIZE

The glue that bonds a community isn't efficiency.

The motivation for corporate growth seems obvious. Companies want to be big and bigger because we associate size with clout, revenue, economies of scale, and—at least in theory—higher profits. In some industries, small companies simply cannot compete. In paper, auto and airplane manufacturing, and pharmaceuticals, for instance, research and development demands enormous investment. But the Wal-Marts, Marriotts, McDonald's, and Hertzes of the world remind us that retailing and other service industries are no less drawn to the power of size than companies in large-scale manufacturing and research-intensive industries.

The pursuit of largeness is driven by a belief that economies of scale always reap a benefit. Arguing that scale matters (just not in the way we always assume), economist Donald Potter notes that superior size has the potential to reduce each of a company's three major costs per unit of sale: people, purchases, and capital. If you can double sales but increase your workforce by only a third, profits increase. Larger companies can negotiate a higher discount on furniture, equipment, and supplies, reducing the cost per unit of sale. They also can keep a larger facility running over multiple shifts, requiring less capital to produce a unit of sale. What this kind of economy-of-scale analysis ignores, Potter argues, are factors such as the speed with which the company can make decisions, respond to shifts in the marketplace, or introduce new technologies. Nor does it factor in the impact of size on the behavior and attitudes of the company's most expensive asset: its people.[1]

In a sea of unrelenting and unpredictable change, huge companies typically race forward with all the grace and agility of a barge. The dilemma for a large company, in the workspace as in other areas, is that it spawns a bureaucracy of immense magnitude. The corporate real estate division of one of the largest banks in the United States learned recently that its internal customers in the bank's various lines of business considered them slow and bureaucratic. The reason was obvious with a little thought. Banks are by nature risk-averse. Their business demands it. The tendency is to analyze every decision, no matter how routine, to death. The value placed on accuracy and thoroughness was captured in one of the bank's core values, MBF ("managing by facts"). Weeks could be spent determining whether it made sense to erect a dividing wall in a conference room.

With accuracy as the driving factor, the corporate real estate analysts spent weeks, sometimes months, trying to get precise headcount figures, which they felt they needed if they were to make a recommendation about consolidating and relocating employees across the company's real estate portfolio. To speed up routine processes, the head of the corporate real estate division implemented the eighty-twenty rule. Nailing down the last 20 percent in accuracy wasn't worth the effort; better to generate 80-percent-accurate recommendations very quickly. Doing that gave the real estate team more time to debate and fine-tune their proposals and projects. Previously, 90 percent of the time had been spent in analysis and only about 10 percent in thinking through the strategic implications and making a recommendation. The eighty-twenty rule improved both the speed and value of decision making. Headcount changed daily and was never absolutely precise. But it didn't need to be. The real estate team could calculate space requirements knowing headcount was in the 80 percent ballpark. Since any solution would allow some flex space, precision had less value than speed.

Order and control make sense in a large organization, but it is the messy vitality of the entrepreneurial enterprise that attracts restless minds at any age, people impatient to make a difference now and not later. I saw this when members of our IWSP research consortium visited a number of small firms in Toronto. They ranged from Husky (a manufacturer of plastic bottle molds for the soft drinks industry) and Alias/Wavefront (a leader in developing multimedia for global corporations) to the Toronto Carpet Factory (an adaptive reuse development housing dozens of small professional service firms in fields such as architecture, marketing, and entertainment law).

The firms were relatively small and demographically young. They occupied rehabilitated nineteenth-century warehouses with high ceilings, rough-hewn wood, and operable windows. Workstations didn't always match. Neither did employees: jeans, suits, slacks, sweatshirts, ties, running shoes, and Gucci loafers sat side by side. The common ground among the firms was their small size, not their business plans. It's useful to remember that the dot com bubble burst because entrepreneurs failed to think through their business assumptions, not because they started small or disdained traditional office space. Their workspace strategies and their size were often the only things that made sense.

In a way, office design is catching up with other changes in corporate culture. Think about what people wear to work today compared to fifteen or twenty years ago. Then, wearing a colored dress shirt at IBM raised eyebrows. Men in companies such as Alcoa and Monsanto wore suits, not sport coats and slacks—and certainly not khakis. Jeans didn't even register on the dress scale. A best-seller from an earlier decade, *Dress for Success*, underscores the radical change in clothing culture.[2] Through the 1980s, many managers were convinced (some still are) that wearing khakis rather than a suit would undermine the organization, rendering it soft, unbusinesslike, and unprofessional. In many companies today, even those we think of as culturally conservative such as Alcoa, IBM, and Goldman Sachs, being businesslike no longer demands wearing a suit and tie. They're worn when the occasion seems appropriate, or simply because that's what someone feels most comfortable and productive wearing.

Why the acceptance of sartorial diversity? The answer lies in hard business realities, particularly in attracting and retaining the best young talent possible. Some people just are not cut out to dress formally. This is why in the advertising industry, for instance, certain people are called "suits" (account managers) and others "jeans" (the "creatives"). Scientists and engineers in R&D departments notoriously dress more casually than the lawyers or employees in human resources and finance. Management's tolerance (though not necessarily appreciation) of such differences arises from experience in the trenches. It takes more energy—and creates more frustration and tension—to impose a single business dress code in every corner of the corporation than it's worth. There's also no evidence that wearing cotton rather than wool or an open-necked shirt rather than a button-down collar undermines authority or drives the stock price down. CEOs who never imagined themselves without a tie and never wanted to see others without them have changed their mind-set about what kinds of clothes make good business sense. It is time for CEOs to also reconsider the style—and the size— of the workspace itself.

Maintaining Small Scale in a Large Organization

What is it about small size, and the flexibility so often integral to it, that makes a start-up such an energetic place? Why does it go against the grain of standardization and universal planning, which is the bedrock for workspace strategies in most large organizations?

The appeal of universal planning, and the centralization of governance and policy that shapes it, is not hard to fathom. For CFOs, it's the holy grail. And why not? It promises to reduce costs dramatically through standardizing and systematizing administration tasks, procedures, procurement, organizational change, training—and workspace. Anything and everything that can be fed through the standardization grinder becomes something that *ought* to be. *Can* and *ought* are not the same thing. But dangling standardization in front of a finance officer is like swinging a honeycomb in front of a bear.

The Hidden Cost of Standardization

Consolidation and standardization are like narcotics for many large companies; they can't get enough. Consider the shared services movement. Consolidation of computer systems and other staff services reduces the number of people needed to perform at a given level. Dow Chemical, based in Midland, Michigan, replaced four hundred financial service centers around the world with just four global centers in 1994, eliminating 70 percent of finance positions. They hoped to cut processing costs by 25 percent; they actually reduced them by 50 percent.[3] A Deloitte Consulting and International Data survey of fifty Fortune 500 companies found an "average return on investment of 27 percent for traditional shared services projects, driven in large part by head-count reductions averaging 26 percent."[4]

Interestingly, the term *shared services* is attributed to Bob Gunn, cofounder of the Boston-based consulting firm Gunn Partners. Gunn is quoted as admitting that "centralization was a dirty word." Shared services, a more euphemistic term, occurred to him in the shower one morning, and it stuck. From an arcane concept buried within the dark recesses of the corporate bureaucracy, the concept has taken hold in all areas of business operations.

Consider "Internet-enabled" self-service: taking all the standardized processes shaped by the shared services concept and ERP (enterprise resource planning) and putting them on the Web. Yesterday's level of consolidation and staff reduction begins, in theory at least, to look trivial. Why hire specialized staff to input HR or expense data to a centralized system when you can require thousands of your employees, whom you already pay to do other work, to do the same thing via the Web? The honeycomb just got sweeter.

But is self-service really service? Is it really as cost-effective as it seems? Web-based services shift costs from a centralized administrative function to every corner in the corporation, but with a critical characteristic: these costs never surface or are counted in the departments where they end up. The department that off-loaded the tasks looks terrific, as do the planners and consultants who made it all possible. But the thousands of employees and customers who now have more unpaid work are treated like a demented cousin; everyone knows they exist but no one talks about them and they are always hidden from view. Jeff Stoll, executive director of human resources strategic initiatives at Amerck and Co., which has rolled out Web-based HR functions such as compensation planning, admits that even though executives love the anticipated cost savings, others raised the question of the hidden costs; "The director of my group is a world-renowned oncologist doing cancer research with 100 people working for him. The last thing we want him to do is sit in front of a terminal and do salary planning. Get some HR person to do that."[5] Shifting costs doesn't eliminate them.

These examples paint a picture of centralization and shared services as the enemy of choice and variety. They don't have to be. Hoteling, for example, is essentially a form of shared service. Numerous people use the same space at different points in time. Online reservation systems make it easy to know where and when space will be available. Reservations can be made with a few keystrokes. No one has to wander the halls peeking in and out of rooms to find a place to work. Because 100 percent of the employees are never in the office at the same time, the overall amount of space needed can be reduced. Not everyone needs to own the place where she or he works. At least part of the costs saved by reducing the number of offices can be reallocated to create a wider range of more distinct and interesting places to work individually or meet with others. Some of the effort in making reservations and finding space is shifted to the individual employees, but in the best systems the employee benefits by having more choice, variety, and better-quality settings in which to work.

A Diverse Workplace Strategy

Centralization works when it mobilizes energy and responds to local conditions.

Several years ago, John Spitznagel, a former graduate student, examined global real estate strategies for six major American computer companies. They all had some sort of centralized design guidelines or standards intended to guide facility construction. The most elaborate manuals, often captured in several weighty volumes of highly detailed building specifications, were not much used ("Well, let me look over here in this locked cabinet. Oh, I can't get in. Too bad I have no idea where the key is!"). The most concise guidelines, which simply called for building "simple, efficient, and economical" buildings, were well understood. They resulted in buildings all over the world that, though not identical, met these criteria. Common principles defined at the top of the organization allowed variety, flexibility, and local solutions for each building. Smart companies didn't force contractors in Germany to use the same type of sprinkler system used in America, at much greater trouble and expense. They focused on achieving the same level of fire safety. The natural outcome of centralization doesn't have to be standardization and uniformity.

Change and Scalability

A legitimate concern with anything customized or unstandardized, whether furniture, layout, or a way of constructing and procuring space, is that as the organization changes over time (as it does constantly) what has worked in one case does not work in another. The concern, if not palpable fear, is that allowing choice and variety, applied throughout the corporation, will be extraordinarily time-consuming, disruptive, and costly. The fundamental rule in Intel's "copy exactly" approach to building manufacturing plants for chips—that there be zero invention or innovation at the manufacturing sites—reflects this attitude perfectly. This strategy may work brilliantly for environments in which one manufactures billions of silicon chips to exacting specifications. But applying the same principles to offices in which millions of people produce ideas, information, and knowledge is like mandating hot dogs as the meal of choice for all occasions because they tasted so good at the Fourth of July picnic. The solution varies with the context.

Universal plan offices, where the footprint or size of the office is the same for virtually everyone regardless or rank or job function, drive down costs because it is faster, cheaper, and less disruptive to move people than walls. They can lead to a work environment that is unbearably dull, and they can fail to support highly varied work and time-activity patterns. But they don't have to. Visit any housing subdivision and you'll note, if you bother to look, that the cookie-cutter houses have invariably been customized in some way. Patios, gardens, decorative lighting, colors, and awnings transform look-alike houses into individual homes. The same can and does happen in universal plan offices, not only with photos and mementos but also with an array of furniture laid out in many ways to reflect different work patterns and processes. Unlike machines, employees are not interchangeable bits of steel working smoothly as long as they are well oiled and properly maintained.

New Models of the Workplace

Employees appreciate flexibility in where and when they work, and they like a distinctive place to work. The Dutch federal building agency discovered this in the mid-1990s as it struggled to figure out what to do with its historic buildings. In the early 1980s these small, often intricately divided spaces were seen as a great liability. Companies wanted enormous floor plates, from twenty-five thousand to forty thousand square feet or more, so they could house all of a five-hundred-person department on a single floor. But to what end?

Companies such as Société Generale in France and the former NMB bank in the Netherlands began to ask what good it was, in practice, to have such large floor plates. Putting a huge department on the same floor looked tidy on a floor plan, but its organizational value was debatable. If the goal was better communication, then much smaller work groups made more sense, since people in groups larger than about 25, and certainly 150, rarely communicated with each other. Faced with a huge stock of historic buildings with small floorplates that it could not easily renovate or sell, the

Dutch government began to understand that smaller offices, with great individual character inside and out, appealed to and raised the morale of its own employees, who appreciated a friendlier, almost familylike, place to work. In combination with sophisticated telecommunications, these smaller historical buildings dotted around the landscape eliminated the need to commute to and from a central office building each day, a human tide rising and ebbing on the conventions of the industrial age. The Dutch found that a great opportunity lies waiting for exploitation by providing smaller, more human scale enterprises. The New Urbanism movement has demonstrated the same principle in the realm of urban design and residential development.

The Power of a Five-Minute Walk

The New Urbanism movement emerged in the United States in the 1990s in response to suburban sprawl and the damage done to both the environment and the social fabric of communities by almost total dependence on cars as a means of local transport. Led by architects and planners such as Andres Duany and Elizabeth Plater-Zyberk, the New Urbanists created pedestrian-oriented communities, among them Seaside, near Miami, and Disney's Celebration, near Orlando, Florida.[6] These small-scale communities are all about size and scale, which New Urbanists have translated into rather precise building rules of thumb: "The optimal size of a neighborhood is a quarter mile from center to edge." This distance is the equivalent of a five-minute walk at a leisurely pace. The purpose is to bind the neighborhood by means of where its inhabitants can walk to within about five minutes for their daily needs: a convenience store, post office, bank, school, day-care center, and so on.

Underlying the five-minute walk is the deep belief that vital communities benefit from mixed-used development, not the rigid separation and segregation of uses that has been the hallmark of zoning in the United States. Duany and Plater-Zyberk argue that "the conventional suburban practice of segregating uses by zones is the legacy of the 'dark satanic mills' which were once genuine hazards to public welfare."[7]

This idea that people need to be protected from filthy and immoral surroundings has roots in Victorian-era mythology. New Urbanist Todd Bressi writes:

> The most powerful icon of the middle-class, the single-family detached house surrounded by ample yards . . . was seen as a cradle, nurturing [and cultivating] the emerging independent nuclear family, and as a bulwark, insulating women and children from the industrial city's evils. The house nurtured the family by providing specialized places for socializing, private life and household work, and by offering an opportunity, through landscaping and interior decoration, for the expression of individual taste. And the house, protected in its residential enclave and surrounded

by spacious yards, offered privacy and protection from outside contamination. . . .
Romantic, picturesque site planing with curved streets and lavish plantings demonstrated the proper balance between nature and human artifice; irregular house forms
like porches and bay windows were considered a sign of organic complexity; and the
yard was a garden that demonstrated the family's connection with the earth.[8]

By employing rules of thumb grounded in observation of cities and communities that
have worked historically, the New Urbanists have succeeded in challenging the thinking of developers around the country. Smaller-scale developments, with greater variation in both building and landscape, evoke images of home and of a way of living
and interacting with neighbors that people are drawn to. For this reason, they can also
be profitable. What is it about smaller-scale communities that makes them so appeal-
ing? In his wonderful book *The Tipping Point,* Malcolm Gladwell suggests that size
and scale are related to our capacity for processing information, and that this affects
organizational size.[9]

The Limits of Group Size

The idea that there are natural limits to how much information we can process has
strong scientific underpinnings. In terms of cognitive capacity, as with the ability to
remember bits of information, the number is about seven. Gladwell quotes Jonathan
Cohen, a memory researcher at Princeton University, who explains why telephone
numbers have seven digits: "Bell wanted a number to be as long as possible so they
could have as large a capacity as possible, but not so long that people couldn't remember it." Gladwell describes how Robin Dunbar, an British anthropologist, has applied cognitive capacity to what he calls our "social channel capacity," the number
of people with whom we can interact and communicate effectively:

> If you belong to a group of five people, Dunbar points out, you have to keep track of
> ten separate relationships: your relationships with the four others in your circle and
> the six other two-way relationships between the others. That's what it means to know
> everyone in the circle. You have to understand the personal dynamics of the group,
> juggle different personalities, keep people happy, manage the demands on your own
> time and attention, and so on. If you belong to a group of twenty people, however,
> there are now 190 two-way relationships to keep track of: 19 involving yourself and
> 171 involving the rest of the group. That's a fivefold increase in the size of the group,
> but a twentyfold increase in the amount of information processing needed to "know"
> the other members of the group. Even a relatively small increase in the size of a
> group, in other words, creates a significant additional social and intellectual burden.[10]

This same pattern, Dunbar notes, holds true in military organizations. Functional fighting units are typically about two hundred men, and they have remained "obdurately stuck at this size despite all the advances in communications technology since the first world war. Rather, it is as though the planners have discovered, by trial and error over the centuries, that it is hard to get more than this number of men sufficiently familiar with each other so that they can work together as a functional unit." Large armies exist, of course. But as size increases, so do the hierarchies and rules and regulations needed to command loyalty and cohesion. Below 150, these goals can be achieved informally, "on the basis of personal loyalties and direct man-to-man contacts."

Variations on the small-is-beautiful principle surface in many areas. Lorraine Maxwell, an environmental psychologist who studies the effects of density on the behavior of children, notes that more than forty years ago psychologist Roger Barker found that in smaller high schools, those with fewer than five hundred students, more students participated in extracurricular activities, had a more positive self-image, showed greater personal responsibility, and were more sensitive to the needs of other students.[11] Similar findings have been found for serious student misconduct. In general, students in smaller schools consistently demonstrate a greater sense of personal responsibility. Of particular interest with regard to the rule of 150 is that studies show that academic achievement is higher in elementary schools with between one hundred and two hundred students than in larger schools. Small class size fosters more voluntary student participation, more positive affect for both students and teachers, and higher achievement scores.

More voluntary participation, higher achievement, and more positive social relationships are not behaviors of value only in elementary school children. The small-is-beautiful principle has been applied by very successful companies, for much the same reason. Gore Associates, a privately held multimillion-dollar firm based in Newark, Delaware, is a prime example . Gore, best known for its breathable water-resistant fabrics (Gore-Tex), also makes dental floss; special insulating coating for computer cables; and a variety of specialty cartridges, filter bags, and tubes for the automobile, semiconductor, pharmaceutical, and medical industries.

The company has no organization charts, no budgets, no elaborate strategic plans. Salaries are determined collectively. Offices are plainly furnished and the same size. Responsiveness to the market, in what is essentially a manufacturing environment, comes at the level of the local plant. Gladwell writes that Gore "is a big established company attempting to behave like a small entrepreneurial start-up."

Success has followed. Its employee turnover is one-third the industry average. It has been profitable for thirty-five consecutive years. Gladwell writes that "Gore has managed to create a small-company ethos so infectious and sticky that it has survived their growth into a billion-dollar company with thousands of employees."[12] They also follow the rule of 150.

As I learned in interviews with senior management at Gore Associates, Wilbert "Bill" Gore, the founder of the company, felt that beyond about 150 or so employees easy and frequent interaction began to break down. To guard against reduction of the interaction and cohesiveness of teams that comes with increasing size, Gore kept plants at about 150 employees, adding a new plant rather than making an existing plant larger in pursuit of efficiencies of scale. In practice, this meant that no plant was built larger than 50,000 square feet. As a result, in Delaware the company has fifteen plants within a twelve-mile radius. The goal is to have buildings that foster an individual culture in each. They don't kid themselves that lots of buildings on a single campus create a single, cohesive organization. Two buildings separated by a parking lot may not seem far apart, but Gore's experience was that once you had to walk that far you might as well get in your car and drive five miles. Just as important, separate buildings promote independence.

The key, of course, is that Gore *wanted* to create independence, and distinct cultures, in marked contrast to most large organizations that strive to create a single cohesive culture (and hope that a single logo, rigid space standards, and a corporate campus will make that happen). Like a living cell, Gladwell notes, "the company has undergone an almost constant process of division and redivision. Where other companies would build an addition or double a shift, Gore split groups up into smaller and smaller pieces."

One reason the small plant, with somewhere between 150 and 250 people, works is peer pressure. As a manager at Gore Associates told Gladwell, "The pressure that comes to bear if we are not efficient at a plant, if we are not creating good earnings for the company, the peer pressure is unbelievable." When everyone knows everyone, "Peer pressure is much more powerful than a concept of a boss. Many, many times more powerful. People want to live up to what is expected of them." By co-locating numerous functions for an entire business unit (R&D, manufacturing, marketing) in the same small plant, everyone knows what everyone is doing and how it all relates to each other. It's not just knowing someone is a nice guy. In a small plant, "It's, Do you really know them well enough that you know their skills and abilities and passions? That's what you like, what you do, what you want to do, what you are truly good at. Not, Are you a nice person?"

Innovation Starts Small

Most firms, of course, reject concepts such as the rule of 150 out of hand. Operating multiple, small-scale enterprises, each requiring its own receptionists, administrators, and facilities, is widely seen as inefficient. At the heart of the issue is "scalability." How much of what characterizes small-scale enterprises—whether a firm, plant, or team—can be maintained as a company grows and expands? The debate about what should be centralized and what decentralized, what standardized and what customized, plays out on this broader organizational stage and begs the question, How much standardization in workspace strategy—the layout, design, look, and feel of an office floor, a building, a site—is functionally required, and to what ends?

Conventional wisdom deems the lack of workspace uniformity and standardization in a small enterprise, from the kinds of desks in the office to variation in their layout, as unscalable—that is, unable to be economically applied at a large scale. A handful of executives I have met over a twenty-year period, most notably Pekke Roine of what was formerly DEC Finland and Lisa Joronen of SOL in Helsinki, have managed to not just think outside the box but smash the box and toss it aside. The same is true of large, global companies such as Accenture, KPMG Peat Marwick, Alcoa, IBM, and Goldman Sachs.

Offices in these companies are notable not for their architectural novelty but for their redefinition of what constitutes a quality work environment. No longer does the way space is designed and allocated presume that most employees come into the office in the morning, go directly to their office, and sit there for most of the rest of the day. Instead, the individual workspace is smaller and more open, reflecting the value placed on face-to-face interaction. Designed with a range of distinct types of formal and informal meeting areas, identical conference rooms give way to a greater variety of settings in which staff can choose to work. Some are open, some closed. Some have traditional conference room furniture, while others offer a range of comfortable and informal seating. Standardization in the design of a particular work setting such as an informal meeting room comfortably coexists with a wider variety of settings available to employees. Quality has been redefined from being a matter of more expensive furniture and finishes and larger offices to provision of a range of settings that support common work activities in a highly pleasant but not sumptuous manner.

Workspace strategies of this kind may not in themselves offer striking visual images destined for an architectural centerfold, but they underscore that workspace innovation isn't the province only of small or start-up companies. Organizational control, and the consistency and efficiency that it permits, doesn't have to be at war with choice and diversity. How space is designed and allocated can unleash the energy, commitment, and creativity of individuals, teams, and departments. Organizations that thrive depend on such behavior. No one, and no team, thinks of itself as a mirror image of another person or team. In a world where the cheapest computer can do more than a supercomputer of a decade ago and furniture is designed to be easily reconfigured, it really isn't all that difficult, for example, to maintain several workstation designs. Resistance to such functional variety may be justified in terms of administrative complexity, concern about fairness and equity, and the need to maintain brand consistency. But more often the underlying reason is that someone in charge believes that lack of standardization is messy, untidy, and unprofessional. Rarely is it based on any evidence that choice and diversity are the enemies of the bottom line.

At least one institution in our society has for a long time understood the value of diversity and standardization: the large university. Universities are big business. They employ thousands of employees and occupy millions of square feet of space, some of it extraordinarily sophisticated. Their most important product is the generation and dissemination of knowledge. World-renowned universities such as Harvard and Oxford have prospered for hundreds of years by developing a few simple controls, procedures, and administrative boundaries within which individuals, departments, research centers, and colleges operate with great freedom.

Though far from perfect, the defining character of a successful university is that consistency and control on the one hand and diversity and choice on the other are viewed as two sides of the same coin. Physically, an academic campus comprises buildings that typically vary dramatically in appearance and physical standards. Buildings are regularly built and renovated, but almost never to look exactly like the building next door either inside or out. Faculty offices differ in size and furnishings, as do staff offices, conference rooms, classrooms, and laboratories. At least at Cornell, how space is allocated is less a matter of rank per se than length of employment. Over time, faculty migrate to offices they prefer as the spaces become available with the departure or retirement of colleagues. The university may be large, as is Cornell University, but it is effectively subdivided into smaller and smaller units, from a college within the university such as Human Ecology to a department within the college such as Design and Environmental Analysis. Each organizational level has considerable autonomy in how it operates as well as significant differences in the space its faculty, staff, and students occupy.

The academic community exploits large scale in its library, sport, and dining facilities, which serve the entire campus community, while allowing smaller-scale enterprises such as departments and research centers with anywhere from 25 to 150 people or so to flourish in their own space, designed and organized to support their own distinct organizational culture and work processes. Few think (let alone worry) about how individual offices and other work settings in these smaller-scale units are not identical. Trying to implement a single facility standard and uniform space standards for labs and offices would ignite a firestorm of protest.

Where others see the jagged and sharp edges of chaos in workspace diversity, top-flight universities have long understood that such diversity is at the heart of what makes them the source of continuing invention and innovation so admired globally. Diversity may, at first glance, look messy. In truth, it imparts an invisible order for dealing with a complex, changing, and demanding labor force. The challenge for large organizations operating across regional, national, and global geographies is to manage size in ways that invite rather than stifle diversity.

Implications for Practice

- Breaking up larger units into smaller ones is beneficial when the goal is more innovation and a more fluid flow of information.
- Create smaller groupings of about twenty-five people or so within a large department or floor plate using a variety of boundary cues. They don't have to be walls; they can be banners, signs, panels, plants, product displays . . . just about anything.
- Boundaries don't have to be rigid or impermeable. They have only to create a sense of community at a smaller scale, much like the distinctions we draw between home, neighborhood, community, city, region, and nation. We know when we are in one without losing sight that we also belong to the others. The military does it by breaking up thousands of men and women into squads, platoons, and on up to a battalion. The smaller the unit, the tighter the bonds, but like nesting dolls they are all part of the same organization.
- Effectiveness trumps efficiency. The ever-present danger is applying rigid efficiency criteria to highly effective groups. This doesn't mean "anything goes," with every individual and group getting anything they want at any cost. It means taking the time and making the effort to understand whether a smaller unit is generating the kind of information flow, knowledge network, decision speed, and innovation expected.
- Create small-size units within units, and then develop policies, practices, and expectations about how these units will share information, ideas, expertise, or support within their own unit, as well as across departments and divisions. Training, recognition, and incentives help create a culture that values smallness while leveraging knowledge across units for the benefit of the larger enterprise.
- Make a clear distinction between scale that benefits from standardization and size (for instance, common software and hardware platforms that make it easy to communicate and solve problems anywhere within the organization) and those that do not.

CHAPTER FIVE

MOBILITY

The point of being mobile isn't to get away from others; it's to get closer to them.

Successful teams and companies establish a deep bond, a kind of intimacy, that blurs the distinction between friend and colleague. James Grose, one of Australia's leading architects, and Rosemary Kirkby, a project manager for the National Australia Bank, typify the core of this kind of tightly bonded team. Several years ago they met around a major building project and are still working together. Their passion for their work and the projects they're working on together attracts and energizes talented designers, engineers, construction managers, and many others who come to work on their team. They themselves live in Sydney. Their latest project is in Melbourne.

For two years they have flown back and forth, getting up at 4:00 A.M. in Sydney to catch a plane for an 8:00 A.M. meeting in Melbourne, some five hundred miles away. No electronic communication could possibly substitute for the bond that's been forged between them on all these trips together. They vigorously debate everything, from the design and layout of workstations and the number, type, and character of all the public and meeting spaces to how the corporate culture will have to change over time in order to exploit the building's design potential. These debates can be heated, but they are forged in an atmosphere of respect and friendship. Building this kind of working relationship with each other and other members of the project team depends ultimately on face-to-face interaction.

Forging relationships of this sort among a distributed work team is immensely difficult, as I discovered personally when four colleagues and I launched a virtual consulting business a few years ago. We were confident we could make it work. We were friends and had collaborated on lots of projects. With backgrounds in interior design and architecture, organizational behavior and environmental psychology, city planning, economic development, and information technology, we brought together a range of expertise rarely found in workspace consulting. Client interest was high. The only problem was that we failed miserably.

The logistical and psychological hurdles of a virtual organization turned out to be insurmountable. One member lived in San Francisco. Two lived in Los Angeles. A fourth was in Boston, and I was in Ithaca, New York. Despite our geographical separation, frequent communication was technically feasible. We all had e-mail, telephones, and fax machines. Face-to-face communication was harder. We tried to fit in meetings when those of us working on the same project saw each other at client sites. But then the focus was on the client and project, not on us as a team. Making matters even more difficult, we all had other commitments, conflicting priorities, and differing aspirations for ourselves and for the firm.

We didn't fail because of physical distance itself, though it sure didn't help. The regularity of convivial conversation at the beginning of the workday, sharing Chinese take-out over a desk at lunch, and having a beer together at the end of the day never happened. Though we'd all known each other previously, not all of those relationships were close enough to establish the trust and understanding required to sustain sometimes trying business relationships. Any new firm's chances of succeeding are always slim; working virtually from inception, they approach nil.

Virtual Versus Mobile

Our consulting group was a virtual team. We had no home base where we physically came together, even occasionally. The Australians James Grose and Rosemary Kirkby, in contrast, were mobile. They had a base in established firms in Sydney. Mobility radiates from a social center, however small or elaborate, grounded in regular (though not necessarily frequent) face-to-face interaction emanating from a home base. Virtual work has no center. The airline reservation agent who works from home every day by virtue of sophisticated call routing software is a true virtual worker. Nearly eighteen million U.S. workers spend at least a portion of their workweek in some form of a mobile work pattern; this figure grew 100 percent over a two-year period. Almost two-thirds of Fortune 1000 companies now offer employees an opportunity to work virtually.[1] Typically, this means working at home one or two days a week, often on a fixed schedule, or coming in later in the day while doing some work at home in the morning. The drive for this form of mobility comes less from the nature of the work than from employees' desire to avoid peak traffic congestion times, to be available for family obligations, or simply to be able to work without interruption for a few hours each day. It's a very different motivation than what drives the Australian team. The former exploits information technology to work apart; the latter exploits mobility to work together.

In both cases employees share documents, send e-mails, talk on the phone, and participate in videoconferences. But no matter how sophisticated the videoconferencing technology, it's not the same as being in the same place at the same time as those with whom we're working. True virtual working is, for the most part, a solution of last resort. It's what we do when all the other alternatives are worse. If a client in San Francisco needs a team that has the world's best security expert and that person lives in Frankfurt, London, or New York, then working remotely via electronic communication can make sense, given the time, cost, and physical wear and tear on the global road warrior.

Sometimes these solutions can work surprisingly well. Alan Drake, a workspace strategist for the Bank of America, couldn't imagine that an eight-hour videoconference with several colleagues would work. But it did. Every few hours everyone took a break. They were all committed to the task at hand and focused on that work intently during their virtual meeting. The effectiveness of such solutions depends on what kind of involvement and expertise is needed. But even the most dedicated team still benefits from face-to-face contact, if not among the whole team at once then among parts of the team occasionally. This is why Drake and his colleague Lynne Rieger, both of whom live in St. Louis, fly back and forth regularly to the bank's headquarters in Charlotte, North Carolina. They use mobility to generate personal contacts in an organizational world where, outside of the smallest firms, it is not feasible for everyone to be convened at the same place and same time.

Some firms are pushing the concept of distributed work much further. These high-tech transnationals—firms such as Trend Micro, a systems protection company—are locating their executives and core functions in different cities around the globe.[2] The goal is to gain competitive advantage by exploiting the availability of talent, low cost, or proximity to customers. So Trend Micro's financial headquarters is in Tokyo, product development is in Taiwan (rich in Ph.D.s), and sales is in Silicon Valley, close to the huge American market. What's interesting, from an organizational ecology perspective, is that this philosophy bets on both proximity and mobility. By co-locating core functions such as finance and sales in one place, proximity is maximized where it counts most: across departments or divisions. When employees need to interact more broadly, they do so electronically using a combination of e-mail, intranet, and instant messaging, or by physically traveling to a site. The financial benefit from this kind of space strategy can be huge. Indian software developers, for example, cost less than one-fifth of those in Silicon Valley. For Trend Micro, the thread linking this dispersed global network is Chairman Steve Chang, working hard to instil a common culture across massive cultural divides. He does it by regularly visiting the company's twenty-two worldwide locations. Mobility bridges distance—but in partnership, not conflict, with digital communication.

Recognizing Stages in a Project

The point at which people benefit most from being in the same place and same time varies greatly. At the beginning of a project, at that most critical stage where the problem is framed and takes shape through vigorous debate, the difference between a team relying on e-mail and the telephone and being together in person is the difference between watching a cooking show on late night television and being in the kitchen. You get something out of watching British celebrity chef Nigella Lawson on TV (though I'm not sure how much it has to do with cooking), but it bears scant resemblance to the real deal.

Studies we've done exploring how leading high-tech companies such as Sun Microsystems use e-mail confirm the importance of face-to-face contact. Sun has every conceivable type of e-mail affinity group, from movies, biking, and food to running and sailing. Everyone uses and enjoys them. Still, people make the effort to come together in real time, in the same place. Electronic and face-to-face interactions reinforce each other. They serve complementary but differing purposes.

Exploiting information technology to work remotely can become an ingrained work habit. It has to be, given the size and reach of highly successful large organizations. At the same time, we need to accept that even under the most propitious circumstances the amount of effort and level of commitment needed to make remote work succeed is enormous. Without intense motivation to succeed, or threat of catastrophic failure, it's easy to slip into a ritualized communication pattern. You call and e-mail, but your heart's not in it. The key to effective distributed work patterns is understanding the underlying work patterns that allow people who are physically remote to remain emotionally connected.

Bridging Remote Locations

Effective mobile or virtual workers need more than the right technology, good training, and the time to learn it. The challenge varies with the type of team one is part of. In a study of sales teams in Fortune 100 companies in the information technology sector, traditional work teams with minimal interdependence and a high degree of stability relied on regularly scheduled monthly meetings, weekly conference calls, and the like. For specially convened task force teams, whose members' "regular" responsibilities continued unabated, just finding time for the task force and scheduling meetings was a major effort.[3] Getting everyone's attention and commitment was like pulling on a mile-long string. No matter how often and how hard you pull, you never seem to get anywhere.

Firms whose lifeblood is innovation, companies such as Gore Associates and IDEO, feed off a lively social network deeply grounded in personal, face-to-face contact and communication. The giant engineering firm Schlumberger's R&D building in Cambridge, England, has offices surrounding an oil drilling platform, so engineers can work directly with production people in real time. Auto manufacturers Ford, Chrysler, BMW, and others co-locate designers and engineers to make communication frequent and easy.

On large, long-term projects this kind of core group is formed by bringing together the key parts of a project team. Architects and engineers, project managers, and client representatives set up shop in a common area, whether it is a war room, part of a floor, or a portable cabin on the client's parking lot. Management consultants working on a three- to twelve-month assignment for a client in Kansas City may live in San Francisco, Chicago, or Boulder. Monday mornings they get on a plane and fly to the client site and then return home or to their own firm's offices at the end of the week. This isn't virtual work. This is thirty-five-thousand-foot, high-altitude, long-distance commuting to ensure face-to-face interaction.

Mobility is often used to complement a company's location strategy. For instance, IDEO's dispersed studios—in Palo Alto, San Francisco, and Boston—are largely self-sufficient; they're not subunits.[4] They stand alone but draw on the expertise of the firm as a whole. Likewise, Gore Associates complements its network of 150-person, self-contained offices with a strategy of cross-pollination. To make sure learning spans all sites, staff from one plant regularly visit others. Teams are pulled together from, say, the Delaware office and go to Scotland with the goal of making that plant the best of its breed. Once that's accomplished, a new team is formed to go to Germany or some other plant with the same product line in order to share best practices and leapfrog competitors. Teams remain on a small, personal scale, but they benefit from the advances made in each remote site.

Academic researchers embrace a similar form of mobility. When I was on sabbatical leave at Oxford University I met two biochemists whose research explores the origins and possible cures for cancer. One was a visiting professor from the University of Pennsylvania, the other the head of department at Lincoln College at Oxford University. The visiting professor had moved to Oxford for a year, bringing eight of his research staff with him to work in the lab in Oxford. The two research teams worked closely together every day exchanging ideas and teaching each other new techniques. It was a temporary, albeit not short-term, interaction and collaboration dependent on the face-to-face daily contact that mobility permitted. Both before and after that year, contact and communication continued via e-mail and periodic but regular flights across the Atlantic. Mobility is the oil that reduces the friction of geographic dispersion.

The particular nature of the mobility depends on the work itself. To check the technical content of a report or get editorial feedback on something I'm writing, I'm happy to send a draft to an expert and ask for comment, even if we've never met. For brainstorming a new research project, or thinking through how to reorganize a department, I'm more likely to listen to the feedback and trust it if I have some sense of the person who is giving it. If I want to debate the feedback, then e-mail quickly becomes dysfunctional. The likelihood of e-mail causing misunderstanding and escalating conflict is extremely high. The phone is better, but not as good as having the person in front of me where I can do more than modulate my voice; I can use touch and facial gestures to give unparalleled richness to the interaction. Where learning new skills is involved, the common pattern of research scientists kicks in: go work in your colleague's lab for a week or a month. You cannot learn electron microscopy by sending e-mails.

Mobility's Social Infrastructure

The concept of virtual work is sexy. Most people would rather work at home on a demanding report than fight rush-hour traffic or airport check-in lines. But what characterizes this work pattern is that it is episodic and voluntary. It complements rather than substitutes for a social home base. Walk around almost any office and, with the exception of places like call centers and claims processing units, you will find half or more of the offices or workstations empty. It doesn't matter if the personnel involved are university professors, research scientists, financial analysts, product designers, or project managers. People move around constantly within and outside the office. We attend team meetings, visit clients, track down an article in the resource center, check the progress on a new building project, stay at home with a sick child, run errands, eat lunch, get a coffee. We're constantly on the move. Sometimes for a morning. Sometimes for a semester. But that's not the same as being a virtual worker.

Telecommuting, in its original virtual incarnation, was all about exploiting information technology to do the same work you did in the office from home or some other remote site. It made sense, except that people who initially were thrilled by the idea that they could work at home often became bored and disillusioned when they were required to work at home regularly. Rather quickly, they realized how important the office was as a social setting. It's where we meet friends, try out ideas, chat, teach, and learn new skills (and pursue romantic interests). What most of us really wanted, as it turned out, was the opportunity to work from home or other remote sites whenever we felt it made sense. We did not want to be told to work at home all the time, or on every Thursday. We craved mobility, not virtuality.

The "Chunking" of Time

The difference between being a virtual worker and being mobile relates to the "chunking" of time. I think of this in the familiar terms of how a family continues to cohere even as kids grow up and eventually (most of the time!) move out of the house.

Think about how this works. As young kids, we spend most of our time at home. As we get older, we spend more and more time outside the home. We go to school, we play with our friends after school, participate in sports and school events, take dancing and music lessons, hang out at the mall. In the United States, a high percentage of teenagers go on to some form of college or university after they graduate from high school. At that point, many move out of the house, initially only during the school term but at some point permanently. We settle into our own lives and start our own families. Does the family fall apart? No. How we spend time together changes radically, though, over this life course evolution.

From spending almost all the time together with parents (as toddlers) to short bursts of time together (while teenagers) to almost no time together with parents (as adults), we chunk time with less frequency but longer duration. When we come together for Thanksgiving, Christmas, Easter, and other holidays we stay and visit not for minutes or hours but for a few days. We focus on each other, tell stories, laugh, eat, drink, and play together. It is a kind of social recharging. Then off we go again, to lead our own lives, keeping in touch with phone and e-mail.

Providing the Social Glue

The equivalent pattern, in the business world, is the off-site: going to a resort or hotel for a day or two where the team can interact without interruption. Formal presentations and seminars are interspersed with cocktail parties and barbecues. Teams develop comedy sketches, go dancing, write songs, play golf, take boat rides. Corporate rituals of this kind define another kind of mobility. They are the social glue binding together people whose physical separation makes frequent face-to-face contact difficult. They make sense even when the physical separation is only a floor or two, or another building on a campus. The team working on the National Australia Bank headquarters in Melbourne believed that supporting this sense of community across the workplace, as an integral facet of the design process, was no less important than the design of the building itself. Cross-departmental sports leagues, a specialty film series, cooking classes, and a series of history lectures surfaced as a means of bringing together, face-to-face, people with common interests. The building acknowledged the importance of activities of this sort, allocating prime space on the ground floor to activities where either employees or the community could meet. The goal was to create social bonds that bridge the physical separation of departments within the new building. The building design itself, no matter how good, cannot achieve this on its own. But design can make it a lot easier.

Honoring Personal Preferences

If competing interests and weak social relationships do not make working at a distance difficult enough, add in the fact that we all have our own communication preferences. When I call and don't connect with the person I am trying to reach, if I'm lucky enough (rare these days) to talk with a real person at the end of the line I ask whether e-mail or voice mail will get the fastest response. I know that some people gravitate to one or the other. Why leave an e-mail message for someone who checks once a day at best, if I know they check their voice mail every hour? Individuals have preferences; companies have cultures. Some teams, companies, and individuals use the cell phone as a last resort; others as it as the tool of first choice. Any organization trading in ideas and intellectual capital should trust its employees' idiosyncratic need for interaction.

Age and Gender Matter

When virtual work involves at least some time working from home, as it often does, it intrudes on and blurs the boundary between work and nonwork roles. For women, some research suggests, being able to choose where and when to work—to be mobile— offers more control over their time and place of work, and that strengthens their organizational commitment and job satisfaction. Men seem to value organizational connectedness more. My own unscientific observation is that there is more similarity across gender within the same stage in the life cycle than there are gender differences within the same stage. That is, young men and young women without family obligations are more similar to each other than men or women who have family and children. Although research provides no definitive answers to whether men and women differ in their reaction to mobile work patterns, what can be stated categorically is that any organization that expects everyone to react to mobile work patterns in the same way is likely to be in for a rude surprise.

We also need to consider age. Younger employees come to work not just with contrasting experience levels but with differing expectations. Free of children and a mortgage, of greater concern than the paycheck is likely to be whether work is fun and engaging. Does it offer a challenge? Can they make a difference? Younger people care a lot about who they work with. Part of this relates to their desire to learn on the job, to develop new skills and competencies they can leverage to gain responsibility and influence so they can move up or out of the organization over time. But just as much, it has to do with the social nature of the workplace for younger people. It is at work and through work contacts that young people often meet their future partners. Office romance is alive and well. For people who have started families and have children the social context of work remains important, but it plays a different role. Getting folks who are, say, twenty-seven years old to stay late or go out for a drink doesn't take a lot of effort. It can be easier to convince a teenager that sex is dull than to get a thirty-seven-year-old with a husband and two children to want to work to midnight with the promise of free pizza and all the Coke she can drink.

Younger employees are good candidates for mobile work patterns. They have fewer family obligations and generally superior technical competency. It is one reason you can find recent college graduates in airports at the beginning and end of each week. But McKinsey and many other consulting firms that send their young people out as road warriors all week long know that they still have to furnish a social net. So regular mobility is balanced by mandatory time in the office—often on Friday afternoons. These are social occasions. People are expected to mingle, talk, share what they've been learning, ask questions, get to know each other. Accenture (formerly Andersen Consulting) has built its hoteling office explicitly around the concept of the office as a social club. It more closely resembles an upmarket coffee house than what we conventionally think of as an office.

Gaining Experience with Mobile Work

Mobile work, like any unfamiliar experience, can appear uncertain and be uncomfortable and unsettling. An early order of business for most mobile workers is getting things under control, transforming the unfamiliar into the familiar. The need for familiarity brings with it a seeming contradiction. Accepting the messy vitality of regional and individual differences, savvy companies are also standardizing the offices frequented by mobile workers. IBM, Hewlett-Packard, British Telecom, and many others expect their employees to move around from office to office, whether located around the M25 circular route in London or in distant counties or countries. An IBM'er doesn't want to show up at an IBM office and not be able to pass through security without signing in to a visitors' book or passing through a metal detector. Once in the building, mobile corporate employees hate having to hunt down a place to make a phone call, ask for help in replenishing the paper in the copy machine, or struggle getting their laptop connected so they can check their e-mail. They want everything to be familiar: easy to find, use, and navigate.

Hotel chains have understood this forever. But the best and most expensive hotels suggest how one can get the benefit of standardization without resorting to the boredom of uniformity. The Regent Wall Street in New York City and the Regent Beverly Hills in Los Angeles are superb historical properties, each architecturally distinct and of the highest quality. What makes them familiar is not standardized design elements, but the impeccable service. The layout of rooms and their design has not been cloned, but they are instantly familiar. We don't struggle to find the bathroom or to use the shower. Clear instructions are there for use of the telephone system, high-speed data connection, in-room fax, and TV-based Internet service. If you have a problem, pushing a single button brings immediate assistance. Familiarity does not have to be bought at the expense of bland uniformity.

Lessons of Hoteling

Perhaps the most widespread form of mobile work is what has come to be known as hoteling. Coined in the early 1990s by Michael Brill in a project with the auditing and consulting firm Ernst and Young, the term reflects the commonplace experience with which we're all familiar: calling a hotel in advance to reserve a room. You tell them how long you want to stay, and they guarantee you a room on arrival. They typically don't tell you which specific room you will occupy, and you don't think twice about the fact that the same room was occupied by someone else before you arrived. All you care about is that the room is there when you reserved it, it is clean, and no trace of its previous occupants remains.

This concept was applied almost exactly to the office environment, initially for people in jobs like auditors, where the person was out of the office for days and weeks at a time (hence Ernst and Young, Andersen Consulting, and other Big Five accountancy and consultancy firms led the way). The innovation was broadening the application to people who were out of the office for good chunks of the *day*. Now the concept could be applied to consultants, project managers, and sales staff. Corporate real estate managers under pressure to reduce overhead costs realized that treating offices and workstations like hotel rooms, where anyone could use the same office at various points in time, would dramatically reduce the total number of offices necessary, as well as all the furniture and equipment in them. Employees could be guaranteed having a place to work when they did come into the office by making a reservation in advance. Presto! Like magic, the amount of space needed could be dramatically reduced.

In one of the earliest examples of what Andersen Consulting (Accenture) called its JIT (just-in-time) office, the San Francisco office quickly calculated that the firm's rapid growth could be accommodated without leasing an additional floor of premium-priced space by eliminating the one-person, one-office approach. Instead, they made available thirteen offices for use by seventy consultants. In one fell swoop they saved more than $350,000 per year. Even better, with this system as more people were hired *absolutely nothing* had to change physically. The only change, essentially invisible, was an increase in the ratio of consultants to offices.

In spite of the communications effort necessary to explain the hoteling concept to employees and at least some initial resistance to not owning an office, large firms have adopted hoteling, as the Andersen case suggests, for a simple reason: money. Workplace consultant Cindy Froggatt writes that Deloitte and Touche has estimated that converting all of the million square feet of conventionally assigned office space in the New York region to the hoteling approach will reduce space requirements by a hundred thousand square feet. "This translates into a first-year cost savings of $20 million (based on avoidance of build-out costs, rent, and operations and maintenance costs for 100,000 square feet) and a total of approximately $66 million when the annual cost savings are projected over a typical ten-year program," says Stephen Silverstein, director of real estate, facilities, and office services.[5] Spare change it isn't.

Our own research suggests that many employees may also if not welcome then at least accept and adjust to working without an assigned office if space saved in the elimination of assigned offices is reallocated to offer a wider range of more specialized and higher-quality shared work space, more and better technology and training, and freedom for the individual to select when and where to work inside and outside the office. In early cases such as Andersen Consulting in San Francisco, the loss of a personally assigned office was mitigated by the fact that the office you occupied under the new hoteling system was identical to a partner's offices. You didn't own it, but you got the best room available. It was like having management upgrade your room when you checked into the Plaza Hotel. Froggatt notes that at Deloitte and Touche the reinvestment in a cafeteria-style menu of workspaces includes five workspace sizes (from 24 to 188 square feet), some enclosed and some not. Individual workspaces can be reserved for up to six weeks at a time, collaborative space for up to forty-eight hours at a time.[6]

Hoteling caught on because the cost savings were immediate and clear-cut, employees did not rebel en masse, and as far as clients were concerned, nothing had changed. Hoteling exploits the real estate cost-savings potential of mobility. But there are other costs. Some, such as the need to provide high-quality, reliable information technology so that mobile consultants and sales staff can access databases and file reports from anywhere, were ignored or severely underestimated, especially early on. Today, much of that technology is being furnished for everyone as a matter of course. It's just the price of entering the game. The cost of servicing mobile workers' technology continues to get less attention than it should, but that too has become rather routinized. As more and more information is stored via intranets that can be accessed from any computer with the right password, the danger of losing information or being unable to continue working if a laptop dies on the road has lessened considerably. The technology itself is far more reliable, and the people using it are far more comfortable and competent with it than they were a decade ago. Compact discs and CD-RW disc drives make backing up data, reports, and files simple, and with high-speed lines large files can be sent and received with relative ease and speed.

Together, these advances in information technology have made widespread mobility possible. The mobility increases the opportunity for face-to-face communication. It also generates more flexibility for the individual as to where and when to choose to do particular activities. They can work from home or a client's office, a hotel or café, or even a small satellite office, as they deem appropriate. For employees faced with a two- to four-hour round trip commute to work, being able to drive to a satellite office within fifteen or thirty minutes of their home is, like the money saved on real estate, significant and transparent.

Making Hoteling Work

Hoteling works best when:

- Staff is regularly out of the office 50 percent or more of the time for an extended period.
- Senior managers are committed to the idea. They make a significant investment in supporting technology in multiple locations and are willing to take flak from employees (and other managers) unhappy about losing private offices.
- The right technology allows employees to access information and communicate with anyone from virtually any location at any time.
- To avoid second-class citizenship, unassigned space (including the total setting, not just the individual workstation) is as good as, if not better in quality than, assigned space.
- Managers consider potential for social isolation and impact on tacit learning; this means developing and exploiting information technology as well as other formal and informal policies to promote sharing social as well as work-related information.

Pushing the Workspace Envelope

There is nothing wrong with adopting a workspace strategy that saves money. But better yet, why not create workspace that reduces the amount of real estate required; inspires and motivates employees; improves communication and teamwork; generates free positive publicity in national newspapers, magazines, and TV; and does all this while increasing flexibility? Digital Equipment's offices in Espoo, Finland, outside Helsinki, did just that.

Pekke Roine, the country manager for DEC Finland, implemented one of the earliest nonterritorial sales offices, about fifteen years ago. They were brilliant. Cost savings of about 30 percent were achieved by eliminating assigned offices, but this was an added benefit, not the driver. The driver, for Roine, was twofold. First, he wanted his sales staff to be as productive as possible. Second, he wanted to use a radical design to position the DEC brand in the marketplace as a cutting-edge innovator in the use of technology to transform work patterns.

To lead this project, he didn't rely on his facility manager or hire the best architects in town. He scanned his own organization and selected five of his wildest and craziest (and most productive) people. The whole group went off on a retreat to answer a single question: What kind of environment would make you really productive?

No one came back and said, "Give me a cube." They talked about reclining chairs, where you could kick back with a laptop and a drink by your side. And maybe some music. They talked about their summer houses on the archipelago, and patio furniture that was fun and informal. They liked the idea of the sound of a waterfall, and walls that were bright and cheerful, maybe with large murals. Some people talked about their bad backs, and how great it would be if you could work standing up sometimes. Sofas for informal conversation, or just as a comfortable place to sit and read sounded good. So too did some regular desks and office chairs. The group returned to Espoo and proposed workspace that had all these elements. Roine quickly agreed, with only one significant additional proviso: no assigned workstations.

Eliminating assigned offices helped Roine achieve his first goal: having his sixty-person staff function as a single team. In the existing office, people formed little cliques of four to six, largely determined by who sat next to whom in a small cluster. The value of unassigned offices for Roine was that people would now sit next to unfamiliar people, and in the process get to know them better. Mobility within the office, encouraged by eliminating assigned offices, was used to promote better face-to-face communication. Finland then, as today, was a leader in wireless technology, and that was exploited to give sales staff maximum choice in where they worked, inside or outside the office, while remaining connected to both customers and colleagues.

Unfortunately, Roine's radical reinvention of the workspace did not survive his departure, or DEC's subsequent acquisition by Compaq and

The DEC Finland "Office of the Future" created distinct activity areas, which employees used over the course of the day and week as their work and mood dictated. (continued)

Employees loved the colors, fountains, flexibility, opportunities for conversation, and comfortable seating. (continued)

The design cost less than a conventional office because the hoteling concept reduced the total amount of space and furniture needed.

ultimately HP. But such innovations continue to influence mainstream design, much like the trickle-down process in automotive technology. Breakthroughs such as disk brakes and then antilock brakes, rack-and-pinion steering, and ceramic materials are first applied in sophisticated and enormously expensive race cars. Today's Toyota Camry and Honda Accord bear little physical resemblance to an Indy racer, but underneath their familiar skin lies technology that was proven on the race track. DEC Finland's influence in activity-based hoteling systems is, similarly, reflected in offices around the world.

Managing Corporate Work Cycle

To create value, whether in an office or away from it, people must do more than follow a procedure manual. Unions figured this out eons ago when they developed the "work to rule" tactic to challenge management without resorting to a strike. Want to see a smoothly flowing enterprise grind to a halt? Have everyone engage in only those activities precisely defined in written procedures and instructions. Effective work requires interaction and shared learning. Mobility can retard development of these communities of practice. When, as an example, in one's corporate work cycle does one become mobile without undermining the constant trickle of tacit learning? Do you take a twenty-three-year-old graduate just entering, for the first time, not just the specific company but the workforce, and make her mobile, where she is often out of the office? How does she master the corporate culture and learn how to apply and adapt (and abandon) concepts and techniques learned in the classroom to real clients paying serious money for professional services? Where and when does she develop the social relationships that help her know whom to contact to get the information or advice needed quickly, or whom to trust to share information or ask a question that reveals her own naïveté, inexperience, or incompetence? If you assign younger and more inexperienced workers in the office so they can learn from more experienced hands, who do they learn from if the more experienced staff are working from home, in a client's office, or at a satellite center?

There are no easy answers to these questions. But the solution is likely to involve thoughtful design of the mobility pattern itself. What is likely to be different for employees just entering the workforce or firm is how they chunk time. Initially, short bursts out of the office need to be complemented by longer periods in the office, more like a few days than a few hours at a time. Newcomers need not just exposure to more experienced hands but encouragement and support in learning how to decode the office's environmental messages as well as its more subtle communication and behavior patterns and expectations—in a word, to learn the culture.

Mobile Work and Organizational Identification

Many employees and employers worry that virtual and mobile workers will slip into the "out of sight, out of mind" mode, to the detriment of the individual and the organization. It is one reason telecommuters flock back to the office during an economic downturn, when fear of layoff pervades the corporate psyche. Few want to be forgotten, or lose the opportunity to remind their bosses of the contribution they make, when decisions are being made about who goes and who stays. One might expect that people whose work pattern is more mobile, and who therefore spend less time on a corporate campus or building with all of the physical artifacts and cues that help define the company's culture, would exhibit less identification with the company. But research suggests that mobile work patterns, though requiring organizational effort and technological investment, do not come at the expense of corporate loyalty and organizational identification.

Contrary to conventional wisdom, mobile work patterns by themselves do not necessarily contribute to a strong sense of isolation and organizational fragmentation. When employees who worked from a mobile work pattern (fewer than two days per week in the office) were compared with those who worked more in office (more than two days per week in the office) in a sales division of a large international computer company that had implemented a hoteling program, no significant relationship was found between employees' virtual status per se and their level of organizational identification.[7] In fact, the researchers concluded that "the absolute level of organizational identification was higher among virtual workers than among less virtual workers . . . the centralized office and the activities that used to be conducted there may no longer have the same level of importance."

Mobile workers don't lose sight of whom they work for, in large part because their mobility keeps them in regular contact with their colleagues and boss. One way to do that is to promote opportunities, through effective workspace strategies, that create an environment in the office intended primarily to encourage and facilitate social interaction when in the office. This turns inside out the common practice of furnishing spaces for individual work and then using some small number of ancillary social spaces in the form of break rooms, informal meeting areas, and so on. For mobile workers, it makes no sense to come into an office periodically only to disappear into your own personal cave.

Mobility characterized by opportunities to maintain regular face-to-face contact with people who are not physically co-located has a long history, and a good chance of succeeding for quite a range of employees. Virtual work, where distance is bridged with electronic communication as a regular day-to-day substitute for face-to-face contact, doesn't. Both mobile and virtual work makes communication more complex and require more skills and a stronger commitment to the project and project team than more conventional work patterns do. Mobile workers succeed against these odds because in a large organization they must; there is no alternative, short of recreating very small self-sufficient units as Gore Associates and IDEO have done. But even then, mobility is a fact of life, as each smaller unit mounts intellectual expeditions to learn what other parts of the organization are doing, and to help the organization move forward by leapfrogging the last greatest strategy. Done right, mobility serves employee, firm, and customer equally. It represents a kind of organizational common ground built on recognition that in an organization larger than about fifty employees, information technology is fundamental to effective work, but not a substitute for face-to-face interaction.

Implications for Practice

- Rethink the "chunking" of time. Explore the possibility of reducing the frequency of your own trips and others' but increasing their duration; that is, accomplishing more on each journey. This can involve saving up visits across a campus or to another building so that rather than making five trips of one hour each, which may disrupt a portion of each day, you do it all in one longer trip. The same applies to longer journeys. One trip per quarter to the West Coast, Europe, or Asia might be longer than usual, so that the relationships formed and renewed on that visit can be effectively maintained electronically until the next one.
- Consider giving people the option of staying an extra day, at the company's expense, to see local sights, visit friends or family, or relax. Particularly when such time is spent in part with colleagues, it has the potential to help develop and strengthen understanding and appreciation of others that may never surface in routine corporate meetings and events.
- Think about and be more deliberate regarding who travels together. Rather than seeing time spent getting to and from meetings as "wasted," it can become productive by encouraging younger staff, for example, to travel with more experienced staff. Opportunities for mentoring and informal development abound.
- Increase awareness among people who are moving (from building to building as well as site to site or city to city) about the potential for using time traveling with others to discuss work-related but not task-oriented issues (how decisions are made in the organization, the values that really drive behavior and lead to rewards and recognition, who the best people are to get various things done, whom to go to for specific types of information or assistance).
- Furnish really good technology. Employees are mobile in the service of the company. For most, whatever glamor long-distance travel in particular may have had ("Hey, I'm going to Paris") quickly fades on repeated journeys with uncomfortable

flights; strange beds; and unfamiliar food, language, and customs. Even short-term mobility within a corporate campus or large building can feel like drudgery, so having the right technology to at least make contact and communication and the ability to work productively and as seamlessly as possible reduces the burden.

- Don't fall into the trap of thinking that office work can be eliminated with technology. It can be facilitated, but its primary purpose most of the time isn't to allow one to work alone; it's to make face-to-face interaction possible.

CHAPTER SIX

FLEXIBILITY

The fastest and least expensive flexibility comes not from putting everything on wheels but from changing behavior.

Uncertainty is endemic and chronic in today's organizations. The reasons reveal themselves in newspaper and TV headlines that mirror the ebb and flow of world markets and the global economy. In 1998 the trigger was mammoth mergers and acquisitions that totaled $1.3 trillion in the United States alone. In 2002 it was massive layoffs, involving hundreds of thousands of workers from what were considered some of America's most innovative and successful companies. Enron, Arthur Andersen, WorldCom, and others, once poster boys for quality and innovation, became bywords for greed, deception, and malfeasance. The year 2003 brought SARS and war in Iraq. We've gone in a squiggle of time from a shortage of computer engineers to thousands of online resumes swirling in cyberspace like leaves on a windy fall day. People who in 1999 demanded, and received, six-figure salaries, pool tables, and free food now search for months or longer for almost any relevant job. Companies whose greatest worry five years ago was how to tap into the billions of potential customers in emerging foreign markets such as China now spend time developing contingency plans in the event of terrorist bombs and chemical or biological warfare.

But companies that survive and prosper under enormous external pressures don't let the cacophony of world events overshadow the daily struggle to develop better products and services at lower cost to increasingly discerning customers. To thrive in this kind of turbulent business environment, managers have been forced to adopt a new mind-set about what constitutes not just good business practice but more flexible and effective workspace strategies that allow them to respond effectively to all manner of situations (Figure 6.1):

- A consulting firm obtains a major project that will involve thirty consultants working on site for a period of six months. The project begins in a week's time, but there's no space in the client's offices for the consultants to work. Conventional leasing and fit-out of space would take several weeks to complete and involve a two-year lease commitment, much longer than needed.
- A pharmaceutical company decides it needs to launch a forty-person team of scientists in computational genomics and wants it up and running within two months. The firm occupies two campuses about twelve miles apart. There is no space available in the North Campus, where scientists engaged in related work are located; neither is there leased space available anywhere nearby. The South Campus has space available, but the scientists worry that locating the new team there will undermine critical communication during the team's formative development phase.
- A premier global financial services firm, where for years concern for costs was overshadowed by an enormous revenue stream, finds itself looking for ways to reduce

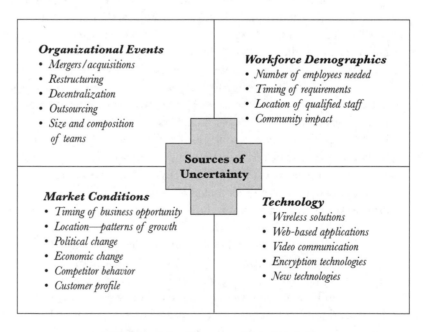

Figure 6.1. Sources of uncertainty.

real estate expenses created by the bursting of the dot com bubble, which drastically reduced its investment banking business. Close examination of its operating costs reveals that the firm is spending $75 million annually because of the churn costs associated with how it allocates its closed offices.

Such challenges don't make the front page of the *New York Times*. But the ability to deliver the right type and amount of space, when and where it is needed, and for only as long as it is needed, is imperative under conditions of uncertainty. Paying for unoccupied and unsuitable space drains scarce resources that could pay salaries, provide training, conduct research and development, launch new products and services, or explore new markets. What's needed is a portfolio of workspace strategies, as varied as the conditions in which companies operate, to manage risk—much as diverse financial portfolios can reduce economic risk.

Yet many organizations are still putting almost everything they own and manage spatially into the equivalent of a standard bank savings account. A real estate and facilities strategy that considers conventional leased or owned space in the traditional type of office building as the *only* acceptable solution for housing employees reduces the chances of surviving environmental conditions that neither of these approaches handles well. You cannot always lease space *on demand* adjacent to your own buildings on a corporate campus. If you want to launch a project team in a month, even if you have the space and resources to construct a new building, conventional design and construction that takes eighteen to thirty-six months renders this option unsuitable. Uncertainty demands more variety and a broader range of solutions (Figure 6.2).

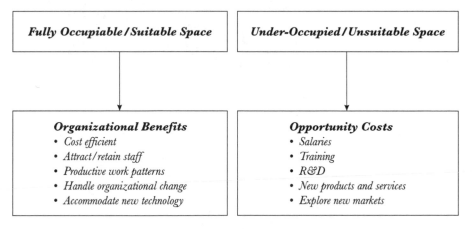

Figure 6.2. Business implications of suitable vs. unsuitable workspace

Diversifying the Portfolio

Monocultures, whether of beetles or building type and office layouts, increase susceptibility to external threats. They create policies and practices that label variety as "exceptions" and then try to stamp it out in the name of efficiency. A distinction needs to be made between standardization (making as much as possible the same) and consistency (creating a predictable process or set of principles that generate outcomes allowing managers to better deal with unpredictability). Large organizations need consistency to operate with any semblance of order and predictability. They don't benefit from every manager and every unit inventing its own processes and procedures, methodologies, or workspace strategies. Incompatible technology platforms, common in the early days of the explosion of desktop computing, demonstrated this at great cost in time, money, and frustration. At a micro level, the ability to organize one's own computer desktop to reflect personal preferences without undermining the free flow of information made possible by consistent and common operating systems reflects the principle of consistency without standardization. It is all about getting right what is standardized and what is allowed to vary (Figure 6.3).

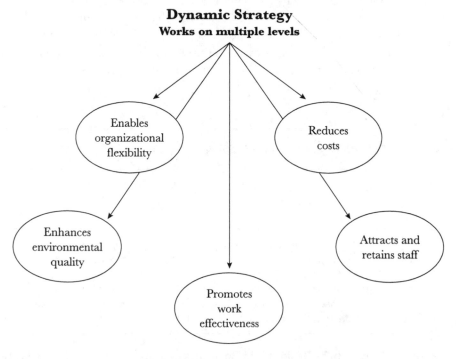

Figure 6.3. Dynamic strategy.

Workspace strategies that standardize in a blanket fashion undermine morale and generate inefficiencies because they ignore meaningful variation in work patterns driven by work processes and market characteristics, as well as the demographics of the workforce itself. Standardization may take the form of making everyone sit in an open plan workstation, or restricting employees' opportunity to work from home regardless of the type of work they do, or the kind of customer and geographic environment in which they work.

I saw this frequently in early adoptions of the hoteling concept. The work pattern of all sales groups was treated as identical. But what worked for a sales group in the Midwest, where the customer base was distributed over a fairly wide geographical area, differed markedly from a sales group in the same company based in New York City, where all the clients were in buildings only a few blocks away. Both groups spent much of the day out of the office on sales calls, but the sales team in New York City came in and out of the office several times a day. Going to another office or location every time people returned to the building generated frustration and wasted time. In the Midwest, where the sales team had to drive some distance to customers geographically dispersed, a salesperson might be out of the office for a day or two at time and then return for half a day before heading out again. Reserving space for half a day or a day made sense. The consistency was in the hoteling concept, but the variation necessary to reflect differences in work patterns was often missing.

Flexible workspace strategies support the requisite variety for a system to survive under a full range of conditions that vary in predictability. Providing diverse workspace options doesn't eliminate all conventional approaches; nor does it incorporate every unconventional building type or space allocation policy that exists or can be invented. It means creating a portfolio strategy at the level of the building(s), and a workspace strategy at the level of interior layout and design, that in all their richness integrate provision of "zero-time" space (as seen in Figure 6.6).

Zero-Time Space

Zero-time space can be procured or constructed and be ready for use in as short a period of time (as close to zero) as possible. It can be achieved physically by alternative approaches to construction, examples of which are explored in this chapter; organizationally, by new approaches to procurement; technologically, by exploiting the potential of information technology to enable remote work; and operationally, by new policies for allocating and using space. Zero-time solutions must meet competing organizational needs for speed, cost, and flexibility while simultaneously meeting employees' expectations for what constitutes a desirable and productive work environment (Figure 6.4).

Policy

- Nonterritorial offices
- Time vs. event paced planning
- Shelling and "dark" space
- Telework
- Mix standard and customized solutions

Construction

- Pre-engineered services
- Mobile
- Tensile
- Modular

Procurement

- Fully serviced offices
- Excess capacity space
- Shared resources

Design

- Anticipate future uses; design for conversion
- Modular (kit-of-parts) and freestanding systems
- Employ highly standard solutions; universal plan offices
- Flexible and fixed zones; service splines
- Mobile and easily reconfigured furniture
- High bay and clear span structures
- Raised access floors
- Software based programmable HVAC systems

Figure 6.4. Zero-time space strategies.

The ultimate zero-time space, of course, is *no space*. Substituting electronic meeting space for a conference room, or adopting an enterprisewide system that eliminates separate administrative operations and the hundreds of thousands of square feet that previously housed them casts the concept of flexibility and speed of change in an entirely new light. *Harvard Business Review* editor Thomas Stewart notes that "if you drive in Silicon Valley, you find the place that is the guts of Yahoo—the core, the center. It's three nondescript servers in a basement, and there's a sign on it that says, 'Do Not

Touch."[1] Cyberspace alters the playing field, but the work still gets done *somewhere* in real space, and managing that space to accommodate chronic uncertainty takes many forms.

Win-Win Strategies

For real estate staff charged by their management with cutting costs, it is easy to focus on short-term benefits of reducing space and to ignore or minimize the downside of cost-cutting approaches in terms of employee morale and the ability to work productively. In the face of the need to accommodate more staff, for example, organizations typically cannibalize informal meeting and team space for more workstations, or increase density to the point where even the most committed employee feels cramped and claustrophobic. Such short-term solutions made in the name of efficiency put effectiveness at risk. Good zero-time solutions work on multiple levels simultaneously. They use space efficiently while maintaining or even improving employee morale and the ability to work productively. The primary requirement for these innovative, win-win approaches is not money or time but imagination and an open mind-set. Hoteling, as we've seen in Chapter Five, is one strategy for improving the physical capacity, productivity, and collaborative potential of the workplace. Several other innovations can have a similar impact (Figure 6.5).

Shelling, or "Dark" Space

Shelling is the policy of constructing the base building shell without completing interior fit-out in advance of needing the space. When the space is actually needed, the time to occupancy is much shorter because fit-out can be done quickly. At Sears's corporate headquarters outside Chicago, the shelling concept was refined to accommodate the fact that managers rarely know in advance exactly where in a building or complex more space will be needed. Sears addressed this issue by leaving some space in each building or floor (rather than in a single building or on a few contiguous floors) "dark" so that it could be allocated intelligently as the need arose. Employees benefit by being closer to their own workgroup or corporate customers as a team or department expanded. Allocating dark space within occupied space reduced the need to relocate an entire department or function to a new building or wing in order to keep them together; or, as often happens, mixing different functions simply because a group has some extra capacity, whether or not the adjacency makes any sense in terms of workflow and collaboration. Here, what might be considered inefficient use of space, since some space is deliberately left unoccupied, works to increase both efficiency *and* effectiveness over time. Time is the hidden dimension that transforms a downside into a benefit.

Workplace *Options*

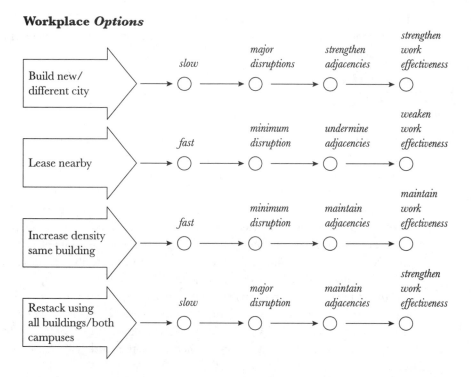

Figure 6.5. Positive and negative outcomes of workplace strategies.

Shelling Considerations

- Useful when future demand for additional space is predictable, but not precisely when and where or for what the space will be needed.
- Additional cost results from providing infrastructure that can accommodate differing and uncertain infrastructure loads (lighting, HVAC, power, water).
- Projecting the need for excess space one to three years after construction is completed is critical, so that excess space is still available at the end of construction.

Time-Paced Versus Event-Paced Construction

Rapid growth and keen market insight allow some companies to expand like clockwork. Intel, the world's largest computer chip maker, builds new fabrication facilities every nine months, before the chip to be manufactured in that facility has been designed. Their strategy is time-paced rather than event-paced. Most organizations wait until a need has arisen and then start considering how to house it. Intel's facility is waiting, ready for use, when the need arises. For Intel, the benefit of having space available when needed in order to increase revenue flow outweighs the downside of building space that may not be needed. The key is that the *probability* of not needing the space is much lower than the probability of needing it. This risk profile drives the decision process. For firms with an alternative risk profile, this same strategy would be disastrous.

Time- Versus Event-Paced Planning Considerations

- Highly predictable demand necessary.
- Significant competitive penalty must exist for being slow to market or for a group or team to become operational.
- Few other zero-time space approaches (for example, leasing or tensile) are available because of the specialized nature of the facilities (such as a clean lab).

Contingent (Fully Serviced) Space

Regus, Carr America, and other companies make available fully serviced or "turnkey" office space. The space comes ready to use, from furniture, computers, and telephones to a receptionist. Originally, such turnkey space served primarily small professional firms (legal, accounting, marketing) and start-ups. In recent years, large companies such as AT&T, Cisco, and Hewlett-Packard have formed alliances and special relationships with such providers nationally to help furnish zero-time space to their mobile workers. Nokia has gone even further, signing a global five-year agreement for the transfer of up to one-fifth of its approximately ten-thousand-person workforce to Regus centers over the course of the contract.[2]

Companies launching a new business venture in a foreign country have also exploited the turnkey approach to occupy and exit space quickly, depending on the success of the venture, which cannot be determined in advance. In a win for three firms, the venerable Lloyds of London found itself several years ago with vacant space in the office floors above their wide-open insurance marketplace on the ground floor. Regus wanted space that it could fit out and manage as fully serviced space in the City, London's financial district, but it was extremely difficult to come by at the time. Merrill-Lynch was expanding its technology services group in London and was desperately looking for space at a time when it was extraordinarily scarce. In the end, Lloyds entered into a business partnership with Regus, making the space available to Regus to rent out, with a portion of the profits returning to Lloyds. They got some financial value from what was otherwise space costing them money, and they could reoccupy the space should they need it. Merrill Lynch got space in the heart of the City of London with a completely flexible lease term (unusual in England, where leases of fifteen to twenty-five years are typical). They paid a premium for the flexibility but could occupy immediately and exit whenever needed. Everyone won. The premium paid for the flexibility to occupy or exit space in a fraction of the time necessary with conventional own-lease strategies makes sense when a high probability exists that you will lose a business opportunity because you cannot establish a base quickly enough, or find yourself saddled with the cost of a long-term lease for space you no longer need.

Full-Services Space Considerations

- Best for a relatively short period of time (less than six months) or small group of staff (fewer than fifty), when accommodated in a single location (in contrast to true "drop-in" office space that may accommodate hundreds or even thousands of employees and dozens of sites regionally, nationally, and globally).
- Makes sense when quite certain about how long accommodation is needed (for example, no longer than three months for a project team, so willing to pay higher costs per month, but only for three months) or about expected duration so that committing to longer lease is not wanted (for example, when entering a new overseas market where there is no clear idea of the extent of market demand or the likelihood of success for the venture).
- Useful when there are stiff penalties for taking a long time to become operational or enter a market, or for staying longer than work demands or market bears.

Excess Capacity Space

Wineries and breweries routinely contract to use excess manufacturing capacity in a competitor's facility. Using the same principle, one high-tech company in Europe sold its building on the outskirts of Newmarket, England, and renovated and moved into what had been a warehouse space less than two miles away. When the company grew, it forged a deal with a business alliance partner located nearby to occupy some of its surplus space at a below-market rate. Both firms benefited. Space was available immediately at a below-market rate for the tech company. Its alliance partner reduced its fixed-space costs and gained a prestigious cotenant. Employees were delighted to reduce their commuting time and work in a comfortable, small-scale, well-furnished office space.

Getting the whole package right is critical. In California, Pacific Telesis (now part of SBC Communications) sent twenty- to thirty-person sales teams to communities for three or four months each year to sell yellow pages advertising.[3] Typically, the sales staff lived in a local hotel, drawing per diem living expenses. Office space in the community was fitted-out and leased, typically for longer than needed. In a pilot project, Pacific Telesis contracted with a Marriott Suites Hotel to give all employees accommodations. They also obtained exclusive use of its conference rooms as a sales campaign headquarters. As a result, the real estate costs for Pacific Telesis were limited to IT, office furniture, and reduced room rates. They paid only for what they wanted when they needed it. The strategy saved money, but it had a downside for the sales staff.

To make the residential solution the office solution all the sales staff had to stay in the same hotel, where the rates had been negotiated with the national hotel chain. Previously, sales staff were given a fixed per diem living allowance. Those who chose to live in a less expensive hotel could pocket the difference in costs, effectively supplementing their salary. Now, since all were required to live in the same hotel, that was impossible. Living in the same hotel had an additional drawback for some of the employees: their comings and goings were too easily observed by their colleagues. What time they came in and went out, and with whom, was far more visible when the whole team occupied the same block of rooms.[4]

Excess Space Considerations

- Whoever furnishes the space must not be viewed as a competitive threat.
- Corporate security (information) needs to be considered but should not a priori be used as justification for why such an arrangement would not work.
- The cost of adapting another firm's excess space can make sense, if its use will be repeated, is relatively long-term, and is reflected in other aspects of the lease arrangement (cost and exit strategy).
- Space does not need to be proximate, depending on the intended uses.

Construction Approaches

Mobile, modular, and tensile structures are three types of preengineered building construction approaches that have the common value of being transportable and reusable. What makes them preengineered is that they start their life in a factory, from which they are transported to the site and erected. Most people think of this type of structure as being of poor quality, or just downright ugly. Telling employees of a major corporation that they're going to occupy a "portacabin" or "trailer" elicits about as much enthusiasm as a cold shower. But like everything else in life, preengineered buildings come in an infinite number of forms, not all of them dismal.

Mobile Structures

Mobile structures have been with us for as long as there have been nomadic peoples. The military depends on mobile offices, warehouses, and hospitals. Every large construction site has mobile field offices for contractors and builders. This zero-time space solution allows a construction team to be housed on the project site as soon as construction starts, and to leave as soon as the project is completed. As the number of women increases in the construction industry, portable units have even been used as mobile day-care centers, moving from project to project to allow women with children to work overtime when a project is on deadline, without having to leave to care for children or worrying about them.

Intel uses trailers when expected occupancy is short-term. They are attached to each other to form an open bay structure to which restrooms, conference rooms, access ramps and stairs, lighting, an overhead sprinkler system, and open plan system furniture are added. All utilities (electricity, voice and data, water and sewer) are brought to the trailer site underground and distributed within the modules. The time from construction to occupancy is typically about three months. These trailer modules avoid the costs of compressing office size and increasing density in existing buildings to accommodate additional staff. Improved operational synergy comes from closer on-campus adjacency to existing buildings than would be possible if the only alternative were leasing available office space.

At Intel cost is not the primary consideration. Speed and flexibility are. But so is employees' acceptance. The solution works on multiple levels. Trailers may not be glamorous, but they offer more space and can remain close to others with whom one works, which makes trailers at Intel an employee-friendly zero-time space solution. They also reduce both the cost and the time of construction, and they can be removed whenever they are no longer needed.

Mobile Office Considerations

- Permitting may take longer and encounter more resistance than conventional construction, depending on the location (for instance, how visible it is to the surrounding community) and duration of expected occupancy. Makes sense to secure advance permitting so speed is maximized if need for doing so arises.
- Mobile units are generally of lower cost than other conventional solutions, even with specialized features (more robust infrastructure, telecommunications capability).
- Conventional mobile units typically are not terribly attractive. If they are moved regularly (as with a mobile medical unit or classroom), this may not be an issue. When appearance counts for more, as it does in a corporate context, clever design both of the units themselves as well as fences, plantings, surface treatments, and common areas such as entrance lobbies and cafeterias can improve the drab trailerlike appearance of typical modular units.

- As much as possible, the interior should be comparable to conventional construction in appearance and the feel and level of services.
- Mobile units create an opportunity to temporarily obtain critical proximity (say, for project teams) on an existing site when any other type of space (leased, owned, constructed) is not feasible or available.

Modular

Several years ago the ABN/AMRO Bank in the Netherlands found itself needing space for six hundred to seven hundred people in about six months' time. No such space was available to lease in or near their southeast Amsterdam headquarters. Today the bank occupies one hundred thousand square feet of class A corporate office space constructed from prefabricated modular units that functionally and visually are indistinguishable from conventional office construction. In its final form the building consists of four floors with a total gross area of about 115,000 square feet (9,545 square meters.). The building is designed to last anywhere from ten to twenty-five years with proper maintenance.

Six hundred seventy-five prefabricated modules created 710 workspaces that are a mixture of cellular, group, and open plan offices. The floors are made of concrete, and the ceiling height is about nine feet (2.70 meters). The data infrastructure is state-of-the-art. The building includes entrance, reception area, meeting rooms, computer room, restaurant, kitchen, and coffee corners. To protect the bank against at least one form of uncertainty, the manufacturer, De Meeuw, agreed to buy back and remove the building after five years if the space is no longer needed. The total project costs were 31 percent lower than leasing conventional office space (including rent and refurbishing). Less expensive to build, faster time to occupancy, and an attractive exit strategy should that be needed rendered trailers highly attractive to the bank's management and real estate group. The real beauty in the strategy, and what makes it a win-win, is that all the real estate benefits gained were not at the expense of employees' acceptance of the solution. Our Cornell research found a high level of employee satisfaction with the offices.[5]

The University of California's Berkeley campus has used modular units in a different way. Straddling the Hayward earthquake fault, government regulations mandate that UC Berkeley upgrade its older facilities to comply with newer and more stringent seismic codes. The problem was what to do with faculty and students in these older buildings during the renovation. The answer was to build a "temporary" quad of modular buildings to be used in rotation by academic departments. Since students could not take a class in the central part of campus and then be expected to arrive in a class in some other part of town where extra temporary space had been found, what became known as Surge Complex was located in the heart of the campus.[6]

This ABN/AMRO office block is made of more than seven hundred prefabricated modules assembled on site.

The interior of the ABN/AMRO prefabricated building looks and functions like a conventional office.

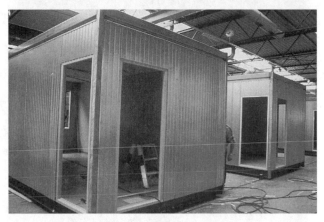

Made in a factory, the ABN/AMRO modules roll off an assembly line
before being shipped and assembled on site.

This simple, modest-looking, shedlike building on the campus of
UC Berkeley houses a modern, comfortable theater. It is part of a
modular workspace strategy to accommodate departments that must
vacate their permanent buildings during renovation to meet
new earthquake building codes.

Contrary to the common view of modular buildings as awful space, the single-story buildings organized around a courtyard were well liked. The university planner described the complex as "almost like a tiny village within the larger context of its imposing neighbors—offering students, faculty and visitors a unique sense of place rather than being housed in separate, scattered, anonymous classrooms."[7] Because the various departments—from architecture needing studio space and others needing standard classroom and office space to those requiring larger lecture halls—will surge in and out of the complex over a number of years, the modular buildings feature three ridge heights, "offering a varying range of spaces, heights, and sizes adaptable to multiple purposes." At a cost of less than $100 per square foot (about 30–50 percent less than conventional construction), the complex took six months to complete, from the start of design to occupancy. The best evidence that it worked from a student and staff viewpoint is that the first occupants, the architecture department, didn't want to return to their permanent home when the time came for them to move out.

Modular Office Considerations

- Permitting process can take longer and encounter more resistance than with conventional construction (just as true for mobile and prefab construction).
- Modular units can be designed to be visually indistinguishable from conventional design and construction. They do not have to be unattractive or totally standardized in appearance.
- These units create opportunities to obtain temporary proximity quickly when other solutions are unavailable or not feasible.
- Modules must be kept clean and well maintained to avoid stereotypical image of "cheap," low-quality building.

Tensile Structures

Like some of their more modest portable building brethren, contemporary tensile structures, with their impermanence, are a form of zero-time space that can be used in a variety of sophisticated ways. The life sciences company Monsanto, based in St. Louis, wanted to quickly launch a bioinformatics research team, but no space was available in existing buildings. It also wasn't clear how long beyond one year the new group would exist.

The temporary solution was the "Bridge," a 7,200 gross-square-foot, tensile structure using high-tech translucent tenting material stretched over a steel frame. The structure had to meet all the same building codes as a permanent structure. It cost as much to build as a comparably sized conventional structure, but from snow-covered ground to being fully operational took just twenty-eight days. Somewhat to Monsanto's surprise, the research scientists occupying the building liked working in a "tent" and thought it was as good as, if not better than, working in a conventional office building.

This Monsanto research laboratory was operational in twenty-eight days.

Monsanto's research scientists appreciated the nontraditional interior of this tensile building.

**The workstations were indistinguishable from those in
conventional buildings.**

Warehouse

Most older white-collar workers used to working in conventional office space think
of warehouses and factories as dingy places, more like their garage than their living
room. Yet if such structures can be made as palatable to office workers as they were
for hip young dot com'ers, they have the potential to be a special kind of zero-time
space solution for companies that cannot predict what activities and types of work will
be done in a building over time.

Manufacturing sophisticated bearings and industrial parts, Igus, located in
Cologne, Germany, wanted a building shell that could accommodate any kind of
use anywhere in the building quickly, even if it meant having office workers sitting
where bearings had been manufactured a few days earlier.

The solution was a clear-span structural system designed by the Nicholas Grimshaw
Partnership. Cables connected to structural columns (masts) in courtyards support a totally open interior floor area where almost any function can be located or relocated.
Panels can be quickly and easily changed from a solid surface to a window and to a door
simply by removing bolts. "Pods," self-contained mezzanine-level rooms within the
building shell, are not easy to move but they are easy to add. Exposed building systems, including the HVAC (heating, ventilating, and air conditioning), water, plumb-
ing, and power and data cables housed in easily accessible cable trays and "drops,"
make it possible to quickly relocate services anywhere in the building, in a few hours

Tensile structures create interesting building forms.

**The panels at Igus can be quickly switched from solid to glass,
from walls to doors, making it easy to adapt the building to various uses
with minimal time, cost, or disruption.**

The Igus building's interior is capable of accommodating office, warehouse, and manufacturing functions in adjacent spaces and can expand or shift these functions easily as the need arises.

to a weekend, without restriction. Modular systems (furniture and interior panels, as well as interior and exterior cladding) use exposed bolts that minimize the need for special tools or labor. The furniture is freestanding and the walls are demountable. High ceilings make possible erecting buildings within buildings to create multilevel space within the same building shell.

The building construction took nine months. Each exterior polyester-coated aluminum panel, simply bolted on, can be removed in ten minutes; an interior panel takes one to two hours. It took two weekends to change the tooling department—with all its machines—into offices. The bearing department, growing between 40 and 60 percent each year, has completely moved location five times in five years. Our Cornell research at Igus found that employees working in the factory/office characterized their space as "energizing" and felt it improved morale and communication.[8] They loved zinging around the "streets" in electric scooters and appreciated the daylight that flooded the space.

The Grimshaw Partnership carried off a similar kind of mind-shift for the call center operators at Nexus, one of the Orange mobile telephone company's call centers. Located in Darlington, England, about two hours north of London, the building is a remarkable warehouse cum office building.

At the time one of the UK's fastest-growing companies, Orange challenged behemoths like British Telecom by providing more innovative products and services along with better customer service than its competitors. For two years running, the J. D. Power and Associates Survey on the UK mobile market ranked Orange number one for customer satisfaction. Costing 8.5 million pounds (about $15 million) to build, not counting furniture and design fees, the warehouse-type building has a gross area of about sixty-three thousand square feet. Its 450 workstations support approximately 520 staff across two shifts.

Why a warehouse? This part of the north of England is economically depressed, compared to the south of England. Orange selected this location because they had other call centers in the area, there was an eager and available work force with a strong work ethic, and wages were about 10–15 percent less than in the south. The problem was that financial institutions and the local planning authority would only approve a warehouse building. With no other service industry nearby, they worried that should Orange ever decide to leave the area an office building would sit empty, generating no tax revenue and having no residual real estate value. They wanted a warehouse—or more precisely, a building that could easily and inexpensively be converted to a warehouse should its use as an office no longer be economically viable.

Fitted out with extraordinary lighting, standard modular office furniture, and more windows than one typically finds in a warehouse, Nexus could be converted to a factory or warehouse in short order because of features such as a standard warehouse floor at the same height as the parking area; access for trucks and materials from the parking area to the rear of the building; and external wall construction easily converted to accommodate large doors for warehouse use. What makes Nexus a zero-time solution was not the time to construct it (twelve months), but the speed and ease with which the building can be converted to a completely alternative use.

As at Intel and Igus, staff knew about and understood the rationale for the building design. The commitment by Orange to create a space that was better than many call centers (including their own, located on the same property, by offering quality dining areas, good food, excellent lighting, and new and high-quality furniture) made working in a warehouse acceptable to employees. It wasn't a perfect solution. None are. But it yielded highly flexible space, at reasonable cost, that employees generally liked. The dramatic nature of the building and its high amenity level helped attract and retain staff and contributed to Orange's branding campaign. The novel design of the building became a magnet for potential customers who visited the space and came away impressed with Orange's commitment to innovative practices throughout their operations.

This call center in the north of England was designed to be converted to a warehouse with minimal cost, time, or effort should the mobile phone company Orange, the current occupant, ever decide to shift its operations and no other office tenant could be found.

Innovative prefabricated structures, as these examples suggest, can succeed on several levels simultaneously. Contract office furniture manufacturer Herman Miller has added an additional benefit layer to cost, speed, and employee acceptance: sustainability.[9] Miller's new MarketPlace building, in Zeeland, Michigan, is a prefabricated system building that meets the rigorous criteria for the LEEDS (Leadership in Energy and Environmental Design, established by the U.S. Green Building Council) Gold certification, the highest level possible. They did so with a building that cost $89 square foot, 33 percent below Herman Miller's typical office facilities. Its operational costs are 41 percent below traditional leased office space. A combination of natural light, recycled materials, and energy recovery systems define the environmental sustainability. The community sustainability comes from a much higher amount of collaborative space and the use of unassigned space for about 25 percent of the employees, encouraging employees to use a number of spaces and get to know more people than those just immediately assigned to workstations around them. Measurement of employee work patterns and satisfaction by an outside group hired by Herman Miller found a high level of employee satisfaction.

What makes prefabricated structures like those occupied by Herman Miller, Igus, Nexus, and Intel viable is that when done with care and imagination they succeed on multiple levels: speed, flexibility, and cost are leveraged by a broad cross-section of employees who find this kind of nontraditional work environment as good as, and often better than, more conventional offices. None of the zero-time space solutions by themselves suffice for large organizations. Their strength lies in how they complement more conventional ways of procuring office space.

Warehouse Office Considerations

- Initial cost is likely to be lower than for class A space.
- Relative ease and cost-effectiveness to convert to other uses makes it an attractive solution when some doubt exists about the market for office space in the future should the business decline or relocate.
- High-bay open space makes it possible to integrate office and manufacturing functions together in a highly visible and interactive way. This can contribute to cross-functional teaming, particularly involving development of innovative new products.
- As with other alternative construction strategies such as tensile, mobile, and prefabricated buildings, it may take additional time and effort up front to win planning approvals, since city officials harbor many of the same initial stereotypes for such construction as do those companies and individuals who will occupy them.

Learning from New Economy Companies

Despite evidence to the contrary, the concept of modular buildings and innovative tensile structures remains a preposterous idea to many corporate leaders, as does the notion that large firms might learn something about workspace strategies from small start-ups. Yet by necessity these firms embody the "act small" decree that corporate leaders such as GE's former CEO Jack Welch argued large companies must understand if they are to be nimble in the face of chronic uncertainty.

Start-ups typically deemphasize status, have a higher employee density level, make minimal renovations to new space, and spend less money on standard furniture elements. Individuals and teams also are given the freedom to shape the micro environment where they work without requesting formal permission or obtaining a work order from the facilities group for every change they want to make. They simply follow a few good rules that protect everyone's health and safety and ensure that prime resources (daylight, quiet corners, outside views, proximity to meeting rooms) are not unfairly monopolized.

At DesignGraphics (a pseudonym for a small start-up software development company), for example, virtually no renovations were made to the firm's leased office space. All the senior managers occupied what was once a conference room. Developers' "workstations" were simple, freestanding desks that could be repositioned by the employees themselves to facilitate working together, or to reduce eye contact when doing work requiring high concentration. The conference room was a couch and white board. Folding divider screens from Pier One Imports (a discount retailer) afforded visual privacy. In place of standard vending machines or a corporate cafeteria, a vendor arrived in the space every morning with a cart from which he dispensed every conceivable specialty coffee. Employees drank great coffee without having to leave the building, and the vendor required no permanent space. Everyone won. The space was inexpensive, change occured with minimal bureaucracy, and employees appreciated the look and feel of the place that had more of a human imprint than many corporate interiors.

The employees working in start-up initiatives of this kind are young. But these are people whom not just technocentric companies but every company must increasingly attract and retain to survive in today's marketplace. Some of these young people may aspire to a large corner office with an impressive view, but few are energized by occupying workstations in standard class A office space. Sitting in a cubicle and imagining how in ten years they could move up the hierarchy to occupy a small closed office doesn't trigger adrenalin flow. This kind of environmental career path is neither fun nor stimulating. What makes employment rewarding for most people, whatever their age, is challenging work and personal recognition for getting it done fast and well. Having cool furniture and equipment is valued, but more to make everyone productive and comfortable than to convey status and rank.

Consider the Eden Project in Cornwall, England, a visitor center for exploring the relationship between plants and people. For the two million visitors to the Eden Project each year, most of the experience occurs in two gigantic geodesic domes sitting on the floor of what was a working china clay mining pit. The scientists, artists, and other staff who imagine and then create the exhibits and events in the biomes and other parts of the Eden site occupy what is called the Foundation Building. Here, guided by principles of simplicity and flexibility, a key portion of the Eden brain trust work on simple, freestanding tables. Exposed computer and telephone cords drape over the back where they can easily be connected or unconnected to power and data outlets accessible every few meters underneath a raised floor.

I watched one morning, a week after initial move-in, as one whole department moved their desks from one part of the floor to another. They had discovered that the location underneath an open stairwell created an unexpected and uncomfortable breeze, so they moved. Themselves. No special expertise was needed. The tables, whose tops were held in place by suction cups and could easily be detached from the two separate sections forming the base, were not especially heavy. The exposed cables and frequent points of connectivity accessed by lifting up a floor cover with no special tools made the move easy. The process of deciding where to move, how to organize the move, and then moving the furniture was not only simple but also became a team-building exercise. Everyone discussed how the group worked, what the problem was with the current setup, and how different solutions would play out until agreeing on one that made sense. The process itself, contrary to wasting time because it was unrelated to their specific responsibilities, developed a deeper understanding and appreciation of what each person was doing and what they needed so as to feel comfortable and productive.

Not every large company needs to look like a dot com start-up or occupy a tent. What the dot coms and start-up world offer us are not their visible forms, the pool tables and foosball games, but underlying workspace principles, ranging from simple and inexpensive demountable work surfaces to leaving a hung ceiling in leased space rather than spending hundreds of thousands of dollars to remove it in order to build an expensive new ceiling with an industrial aesthetic.

The dot com principle of workspace design is making creative use of what exists. It can be applied with appropriate variations in large companies as well as start-ups. Simple, well-designed components used with imaginative, adaptive reuse of the existing environment avoid putting up with an underperforming workspace because the cost of replacing it with an entirely new one is too high or means spending more money than necessary on aspects of the workspace that employees often don't care a lot about.

Value for Money

The British talk about getting "value for money"—getting the most from what you pay for. The worst of all worlds is spending lots of money, whether on a specific location, particular building, the look and feel of the office, or furniture and fit-out, and ending up with something that doesn't work. Employees don't like it, customers don't notice it, it's not flexible, and it costs more than a more effective, but perhaps simpler, alternative. It happens all the time. One of the world's largest technology companies recently spent a million dollars in more than twenty projects around the world to spruce up and improve the look and feel and image of facilities they recognized as being a bit tired. The idea was to spend as little money as possible for the greatest effect. A good idea, but employee surveys done after the changes showed that employees didn't notice much change. It is not because small, directed changes cannot make a difference. They can. But they have to be targeted at what employees really care about, not what workspace planners think or hope are things that they should or might care about.

This takes some time and effort. As part of a National Science Foundation study we did just that at Cornell, more than twenty-five years ago in a local hospital. Originally designed and used as a tuberculosis asylum, many years later it had become a general hospital that over time grew dark, dreary, and dysfunctional. Using old but attractive furniture stashed in the back of storage rooms to improve the comfort of dayrooms, inexpensive materials like cork board to dampen sound and set up a tack space in nursing stations, and colorful curtains in patient shower rooms so that patients in wheelchairs could be wheeled right into the shower, we attacked problems patients and nurses really cared about. At little cost, these changes improved morale, increased interaction among patients in dayrooms, and enhanced the perceived level of health care.[10]

A similar kind of targeted design change, with concomitant results, occurred in an international food company about the same time as we did the hospital project. In one of their older facilities, several million dollars was spent replacing old-fashioned desks with modern workstations, each of which cost about $4,000. The new, more ergonomic furniture had been justified by the expected surge of employee satisfaction with their new work environment. Yawn. No one cared much. Then one of the planners decided to do something we had suggested: give each of the 250 employees $100 to spend on anything they wanted for their own workstation: waste basket, task light, little rug, picture, desk accessory, whatever. The same employees who had expressed little enthusiasm for their new workstations were absolutely delighted.

The principle common to all these examples is to spend money where it generates results you care about. This requires taking the time to understand what the target population notices and cares about, and making the effort to learn if a workspace change succeeds or not, and why. One could easily conclude (falsely in the case of the technology company that spent a million dollars remodeling) that it doesn't pay to try to improve the work environment with small, targeted expenditures. One might also argue that customers will consider the entity disorganized and unprofessional if they see computer and telephone cables draped over the back of a table. Perhaps. Or they might think that the company is inventive and creative, and spending money where it makes the most sense.

In our homes, we make changes constantly, in line with our resources. We do things even when we don't have massive amounts of money for major renovations, new furniture systems, or a new house. We target our interventions. The key is knowing where to invest. Zero-time space solutions of the sort described earlier are not *the* answer in themselves. They make sense as part of an overall strategy of creating more diverse workspace solutions. Though not often thought of this way, they are a form of risk management because they help organizations quickly and effectively respond to and exploit new opportunities as they emerge, without betting the house on a single, inflexible solution.

Career and Workplace Cycles: A Natural Trajectory

As mentioned in Chapter Five, in the natural trajectory of our personal and family cycle we move from an apartment to a small house and then to a larger house before we begin to scale back our home as children leave and we once again become more mobile and independent. This concept can be applied to the workplace. Why force young married couples with children who want to live in the suburbs to endure a long commute to an office in the city? Why require young single employees who want to live in hip areas in the city to commute to, or live in, the suburbs they find dull and stultifying?

From this vantage point, locating an IT group staffed with a high percentage of young people in a converted warehouse in a light industrial area might be not only less expensive but more attractive to these staff than occupying conventional office space in the heart of the financial district. The latter is more likely to work for married employees with young children. Concerns about inadvertently creating second-class citizens by housing some staff in different space from others are likely to disappear if that "different" space is considered by its occupants as better than what they would be entitled to or receive using conventional ideas about what constitutes office quality.

The Pattern Counts

Every workspace strategy involves trade-offs. Modular structures are quick to construct, but they have less residual value than conventional construction. Tensile and modular structures can be disassembled and relocated, but the permitting process may require extra time and effort. Fully serviced offices make immediate occupancy and exit possible but are often not located exactly where the company wants space. The high density of a dot com makes informal communication impossible to avoid, but it can make concentration difficult. The deliberately noncorporate look and feel of Eden's offices help attract the kind of employee required to get that type of work done but may repel older employees accustomed to conventional office design. Why choose one way of working over the other, and in the process alienate some significant portion of the workforce (Figure 6.6)?

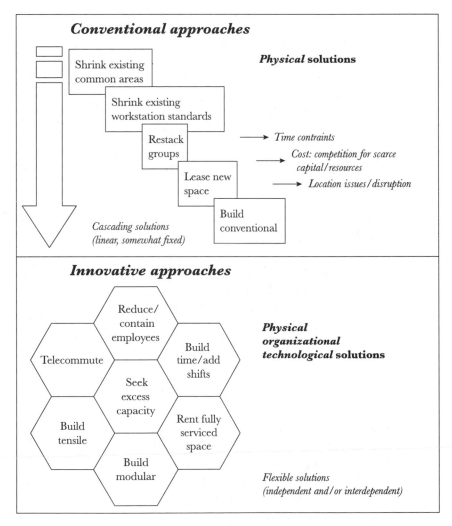

Figure 6.6. Conventional and innovative workplace options.

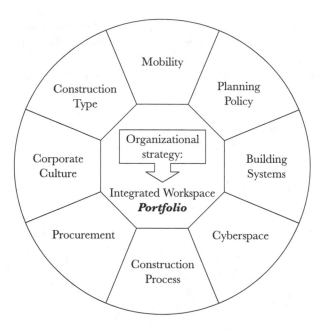

Figure 6.7. Elements of an integrated portfolio strategy.

An integrated portfolio of workspace strategies (Figure 6.7) is a form of biodiversity: it supports a workspace gene pool with sufficient variety to flourish in the face of demographic diversity within the employee population, uncertain market and corporate events, the unrelenting advance of technology, and continuing shifts in the regulatory environment. For a risk-averse organization, a recyclable tensile structure, space convertible to other uses, and other zero-time solutions developed as *part of a diverse workspace portfolio* act as a form of environmental safety net. The bottom line is that cost, flexibility, speed, and effectiveness become part of a single, coherent strategy.

Implications for Practice

- Don't rely on a single solution to serve a variety of flexibility demands.
- Don't assume that certain approaches for achieving flexibility won't work because they deviate too far from current practice. They might not be acceptable if implemented in their standard, almost stereotypical form (prefab buildings), but if developed with imagination and care they may be indistinguishable from more conventional approaches.

- Barter funding for innovation. Seek active collaboration and partnerships with innovative product and service providers. Ask them to develop, modify, and adapt existing solutions to your needs. The firm benefits from what are in effect customized solutions that meet its needs. The vendor benefits from having developed solutions that are likely to meet the needs of the marketplace, and from having a respected corporate user they can refer to in their marketing of these new solutions.
- Explore how underused space of business partners and others can be exploited to the advantage of all parties by sharing the space or subleasing it in innovative lease or profit-sharing arrangements.
- Find and develop solutions that simultaneously achieve highly valued corporate objectives such as cost, speed, suitability, and acceptability. Don't start from a mindset that high quality or speed is always incompatible with low cost.
- Test more radical and innovative solutions on a small scale to develop experience with these more unfamiliar approaches, and to develop working relationships with vendors whom you know and can depend on when you want to implement solutions more widely.

PART TWO

GUIDELINES FOR IMPLEMENTATION

CHAPTER SEVEN

GETTING STARTED

The only shock more jolting than finding out what people really think of their existing workspace or a new one is finding out the same information after it's too late to change directions.

Nothing can quite so quickly expose how an organization actually functions and what it values as an analysis of space and how it is allocated, used, and managed. Where does the organization put its money? Public spaces or backstage work areas? Does it invest in status, with management at the top of the tower in palatial offices and drones at the bottom in workstations the size of a large box? What's the cafeteria like? Are there break rooms or fitness facilities? Where are executive offices located, and how accessible are they? What does an individual have to do to get a new piece of furniture for a workstation, or to reconfigure it? Where does informal communication occur? How long does it take to process a workspace change order? In a major renovation or new building project, what role did the CEO, department heads, and rank-and-file staff play? The ecology of the organization is an open book waiting to be read.

Done with imagination, one of the great benefits of exploiting the physical environment as a communication medium is that its physical presence conveys and reinforces organizational messages nonstop, without effort. Like other forms of nonverbal communication, the message is often given more credence because it is seen as less directly under the conscious control of its sender. Just as good communicators learn how to project their body image, tone of voice, and speech cadence, so can organizations learn to communicate more effectively through and with their physical environment. With speech, the content counts, but so does how you say it. Try saying "I love you" to someone with all the passion and verve you use to wish the checkout clerk at the supermarket to "Have a nice day." Then, duck. The same potential for miscommunication happens when we plan and design workspace.

Analysis of an organization's ecology offers an untapped resource for gauging the amount and kind of effort it will take to bridge old and new cultural patterns. This kind of organizational analysis, or *cultural audit*, needs to happen *before* launching any new workspace strategy. After conducting such an audit, managers can take several action steps to implement an effective workspace strategy: a review of the organization's broader strategic goals, refining a workspace design by approaching employees as customers, and finally implementing a new design through selected pilot projects. In this chapter we examine each of these steps.

Conducting a Cultural Audit

Can you imagine starting a major building renovation, where you are responsible for developing a realistic budget and schedule, without completing an engineering feasibility study? Just when you thought you were on schedule, you might discover that the HVAC system lacked sufficient capacity, and a new one—which could take months to deliver and install—has to be ordered. But that is just what happens all too often with new workspace strategies. The project team plunges ahead, assuming there are no social, psychological, or political potholes in the road ahead.

A cultural audit helps managers avoid those potholes. It puts boundaries around what kind of change is feasible, in what amount of time, requiring what amount of effort. It can uncover the social, psychological, or political hurdles—and the often unstated assumptions of senior executives—that can determine whether a new workspace strategy succeeds. Ultimately, a cultural audit saves time and minimizes the risk of launching an expedition into territory that the organization is unprepared or unable to handle. My own experience with an agency of the federal government illustrates just how valuable a cultural audit can be.

Uncovering Hazards in the Field

My consulting firm was hired to lead an effort to implement a new workspace strategy that included everything from unassigned offices, team areas, and a universal workstation footprint to satellite offices. The intent was to use this location, involving about 550 employees in two sites, as a pilot project that would generate the experience and confidence to roll out more productive workspace designs for this agency throughout the country. We knew that we needed a receptive group for this initial effort.

Our first mistake was assuming that if we could identify a site whose senior management was receptive to the project, their interest and enthusiasm would be reflected in the staff's own attitudes. We relied on the director of national real estate, a thirty-year veteran of government bureaucracy, to select the site. He selected an office in Milwaukee, Wisconsin, in part because he was a friend of the director there. He himself felt comfortable working with this director and knew that the latter was eager to try something new. Having worked almost exclusively in the private sector, in nonunionized corporations, we didn't spend much time examining the relationship between the director and his employees. This was a mistake of the first order.

As is true of much government service, employees were part of a national union. We asked in a perfunctory sort of way whether the union was open to the project. The director said yes, so we just kept moving forward. We never met at the beginning of the project with the local union leaders themselves, to learn their view of not just the proposed project but their local management. Nor did we explore divisions and tensions within the local union itself. We assumed everyone would support the project. After all, we were convinced that the proposed changes would improve employee working conditions and flexibility, result in far better technology, and save real estate costs by using space more efficiently and imaginatively. All of this was actually true, but given what turned out to be the union's deep mistrust of management it was hardly self-evident. We had no inkling, when we started, of the depth of this mistrust, nor how far its tentacles reached.

We gradually came to understand that union-management relations at the national level were horrible. Our project came at a time when federal employees were facing what was for them the unfathomable prospect of an RIF, or reduction in force. Having little ground on which to battle the RIF mandate directly, the union's national leadership looked wherever it could to project an image of strength. Our project got caught in the crossfire of this larger political conflict. The union was the reef lying just below the surface waiting to snag any passing consultant and sink any innovative project.

As part of their efforts to derail the project, the union's national leader involved the local congressman (who contacted the local mayor) to enlist his help in derailing the project. Congressional mandates existed that contradicted each other (some said government offices should retain a presence in the central cities to help stem suburban outflow; others said government should be more responsive to its customers, many of whom had moved or were increasingly expected to move to suburbs). The local congressman opposed the project on the grounds that the proposed strategy would abandon the downtown. This wasn't true, but dispassionately exploring the project's impact on the community wasn't high on the agenda for the union or the congressman.

A culture audit—which we did too late to save the project—would have identified the level of resistance to change and suggested remedies for the problems found. With the benefit of an audit, we would have spent time up front working out detailed communication and decision processes and making sure everyone agreed, *in writing,* to them before the project formally got under way. Or we might have concluded that there was no point launching the project until union and management tensions eased. This was in fact what was favored by a federal mediator brought into the project about halfway through.

Deferring a project, or fundamentally redefining its scope and aspirations, is a legitimate outcome of a culture audit, as it is for an engineering feasibility study. If the audit reveals that management is unwilling to seriously challenge some current practices or resolve issues that threaten the success of the project, this has to be considered from the beginning. If the schedule and budget are unrealistic, and the right people are not assigned to the project, then everyone will ultimately benefit by using these early decisions to discuss, rethink, and possibly redefine just what the project is trying to achieve. Better to scale back aspirations than to raise expectations that are unlikely to be met.

The culture audit can be done by the same firm that leads the project. In effect, the audit is simply the first step in the overall project process. The key is that the desire to push ahead with a project not interfere with the analysis of project feasibility. This includes the possibility that managers may have to redefine the scope of the project, in size or duration; or they may have to bring in other kinds of expertise to maximize its chances of success. As is almost always the case, the best approach for conducting the culture audit uses a variety of data collection techniques.

A useful starting point is interviews with a range of key informants, people like senior managers, union leaders, and active participants in employee groups who really know the organization. In addition to interviews, any written documentation related to similar projects and how they fared are worth reviewing. Walking around and taking the pulse of the place by observing how space is used (or not), who is or is not using it, what is on bulletin boards, and the kinds of adaptation people have made to the space (from personalization to jury-rigged fixes like cardboard taped to a computer screen to eliminate glare) are invaluable clues to the spirit, culture, and condition of the firm.

Reassessing Expectations

During the audit process, executives must assess their stated and unstated goals for the new workspace. In a project with an international bank headquartered in London, I conducted a series of executive interviews to take the organization's pulse about key values and aspirations. The project consolidated employees in fifteen buildings of varying quality and cost into a new headquarters tower at Canary Wharf in London's reclaimed docklands. The stated reason for the move was to help transform a venerable but rather stodgy company into one more integrated and nimble. The CEO's first and most concrete building decision, other than to determine the building's location, was to create an exclusive high-end executive floor right at the top of the building.

Building a stronger brand image and using the building to put a line in the sand about the need for new and more integrated organizational strategies with fewer departmental silos can make sense. But the environmental language of the earliest decisions conveys more about the organization leaders' depth of commitment to change than any town hall meeting, project newsletter, or press release.

The executive interviews I conducted early in the design process as part of a culture audit reinforced the need for the company to come to grips with its operational aspirations. If they were to get a nice new building that worked well without challenging existing work patterns and corporate culture, then that would suggest one project path. If they were to use the building to help forge a new culture and work patterns, that suggested another and more arduous path. No one wanted to confront the CEO on these conflicting directions. So money and time was spent as though it were the former, despite almost all signs that it was not. Two years later this company moved into a new and well-designed building, but one not particularly innovative either architecturally or organizationally. Without doubt, it is an improvement over the previous accommodation in terms of the quality of the environment itself. That's good, but it falls far short of creating a building that helps reinvent the company's culture, change its image, or affect how it functions in the marketplace. There is nothing wrong with this, necessarily. But seriously debating, at the highest levels of the company, the tensions, contradictions, and opportunities for change the culture audit suggested would have saved the company time and money and allowed the project to succeed on its own terms, rather than fall short of its stated goals.

In sharp contrast, when he became chairman and CEO of Alcoa, former treasurer secretary Paul O'Neill's first decision sent a decisive message about his aspirations. O'Neill moved himself and his management team from just the kind of swank executive floor the London firm was creating in its new building to an open plan environment with a kitchen as its social hub. His actions left no doubt that he was serious about transforming the culture. The new corporate headquarters reflected a commitment to change in just about every aspect of its design, from building a much smaller headquarters with more staff based in the field to using technology and space design to support mobile work patterns within the building. O'Neill eliminated plush executive offices in favor of the same small open plan workstations for everyone.

The culture audit helps define the activities that need to be built into the change process for it to have a chance to succeed. Typical events such as town hall meetings and newsletters may mean little in some settings and carry a lot of weight in others. When product visionaries such as Steve Jobs address the troops and exhort them to build the world's next greatest product, employees stampede to meet the challenge. In other companies with a less charismatic leader, less formal and scripted events may have a bigger impact. There is no magic wand. But too much organizational effort, energy, and money is spent on these supporting activities to leave them to guesswork, or to emerge in a sporadic, ad hoc manner.

Aligning Workspace Strategy with Business Strategy

With a clearer understanding of the cultural and organizational landscape and of their own aspirations, executives can fashion a workspace strategy that better supports their business strategy. The workspace strategy must offer flexibility amid uncertainty, as described in Chapter Six, and be a base for collaborative innovation. Leaders in business thinking in recent years have advanced complexity theory and biological models of organization as a strategic framework for companies operating in changing times.[1] In the context of the workspace, five core principles constitute a framework in which flexibility and collaboration can occur:

1. Allocate space primarily in terms of function, not rank and status. Rooms of differing size reflect the need to accommodate equipment of various sizes and types, or specialized functions, not that the occupant is a vice president or analyst.
2. Locate closed rooms around the core, not the perimeter, of the building. This preserves access to natural daylight for everyone.
3. Provide the technology infrastructure necessary to support mobile work patterns within and outside the office. Being able to work anywhere, at just about any time, has become (in the context of a global economy, with its time zones) just a matter of sound business practice.
4. Exploit modularity in rooms and workstations. Today's office may need to become tomorrow's conference room. Common modular building blocks make expanding or shrinking the size of a room, or changing its function, simple and cost-efficient.
5. Specify furniture that allows employees themselves to rearrange it. Teams grow and shrink. Sometimes people want to work alone, to concentrate. Sometimes they need fifteen minutes for a quick chat. Mobile furniture puts the space to work for the people occupying it, rather than the workspace design's idiosyncrasies dictating how people should work.

A European financial services firm used these principles to move from a universal "design solution" for their worldwide offices to a far more flexible approach grounded in and reflecting cultural variations across the firm's sites globally. The leaders realized that managing directors in London didn't need to have offices the same size as those in Tokyo or Frankfurt. Conference rooms could vary in size, look, and feel. Decisions of this sort, taken within the framework of the workspace principles, generate naturally the requisite variety to support the diversity that existed everywhere in the company. The result is not a weak compromise solution eliciting apathy (if not

Union Carbide's same-size office modules could be used for a single office, a conference room, or an informal meeting area simply by changing the furniture.

resentment) but a stronger, more resilient, self-regulating process with the potential to evolve in response to unpredictable events and opportunities.

Questions for Setting Workspace Strategy

With broad strategic principles in mind, managers can dig deeper to identify specific workspace needs. Organizations and project leaders need to be able to answer some basic questions:

- How many employees do we have in workgroups, and where are these groups located (what city, campus, building, floor)?
- What is the density (usable square footage per person) of each group, and how does it vary across groups, buildings, and locations?
- How many more people could a given building or space accommodate before it became dysfunctional? How do we define and measure *dysfunctional*?
- What is the probability that headcount projections are accurate? How accurate have they been in the past for various divisions, departments, and teams?
- What is the probability distribution of lease or sublet costs rising a given amount for a particular area over a period of five, ten, or fifteen years?
- What is the cost of turnover per employee, and what percentage of employees have left in the various groups *and different buildings and parts of buildings* in the last one to three years?
- What's the probability that moving to a less costly and less desirable location will increase employee turnover?

Without answers to questions like these, it is impossible to develop any workspace strategy, let alone an agile one.

To deal with chronic uncertainty executives need information that goes far beyond headcount. They need to understand—and to explicitly debate—the likelihood of various events occurring and their presumed effect on the business. From the discussion thoughtful decisions about the workspace can emerge, even amid uncertainty. Exercises such as scenario planning can help managers envision plausible alternative futures. The question remains, In what form, and how diverse, should the workspace strategy be? An integrated portfolio approach that employs both conventional and alternative workspace solutions offers the best defense against uncertain conditions. In this kind of strategy a prefabricated office building like the one ABN/AMRO Bank built outside Amsterdam isn't meant as the default solution every time space is needed, nor is the tensile structure Monsanto built in St. Louis. But both make it possible, in a way conventional construction or leasing could not, to meet a pressing organizational need quickly and at acceptable cost.

Knowing Your Workspace Customer

Business managers, the people responsible for developing and bringing to market new products and services (the internal workspace customer), regularly complain that the facility management or real estate group responsible for supporting their workspace needs doesn't understand them. Yet if you talk with their facilities management and real estate groups they are more committed than ever to listening to and understanding the voice of the customer. What's going on? The answer lies in what is meant by understanding the customer and how one goes about doing that.

Understanding the customer isn't the same as giving customers whatever they want, especially if that undermines the broader corporate mission. Consider the business manager who decides that she wants the real estate group to find her an additional ten thousand square feet of space in the current location to accommodate growth in her unit, or to spend several hundred thousands dollars upgrading her unit's space to a higher standard. It may make sense for that group. But if the broader corporate strategy is to shift out of that market to other cities with a better long-term employee base projection, then the business investment rationale that works for the individual unit quickly loses value in the context of the enterprise as a whole. To help the business unit meet its current business requirements, a real estate team needs to enter into a dialogue with the business unit to seek solutions that work for both it and the enterprise as a whole. This might mean adopting some form of smaller workspace standard or hoteling for an interim period, until a long-term solution can be implemented, in order to accommodate growth in the geography in the short run without leasing additional space.

To understand the customer well, you need to discover the *governing* issues—those that are deeply held and actually drive employee behavior and attitudes. It's a bit like oil exploration; the geologist knows the oil is down there somewhere, but it can be hard to find, with a lot of false leads along the way. The lawyer who says she requires privacy and thus needs a closed office may be talking in code more about status than confidentiality. The supervisor who warns against mobile work because it could undermine teamwork may be as concerned about the transformation of his managerial role as about the decreased flow of communication. Understanding the customer means exploring these issues to a point where you can confidently distinguish between governing and surface issues.

From this perspective, understanding the customer means knowing:

- Not just what goals people want to achieve but also knowing how they work—or could work with new information technologies, the right training, and supportive management policies and practices
- That satisfying one customer without alienating another requires finding common ground in larger corporate values and goals

- The broader range of issues that create real or perceived barriers to sharing information or accepting new ways of working (such as fear of job loss, or career stagnation); it's not just the daily work patterns and processes that count
- What employees consider *incentives (and disincentives)* for working in new ways
- How to generate creative solutions that support customer work requirements without necessarily maintaining the status quo

Focusing the discussion exclusively on so-called functional requirements can turn into a shell game where everyone works hard to keep everyone else from looking in the right place. What's needed is leadership that has the vision and gumption to uncover governing issues, address them, and find creative solutions for them.

Launching Pilot Projects

No matter how much time and effort a company devotes to culture audits and workspace analyses, at some point managers are always left with this alarming truth: "We've never done this in *our* company before, and we don't really know how it will work." There really is only one answer: build it. Full-scale mock-ups and pilot projects are the kind of company-specific experience for which there is no substitute. They cost money, but they often constitute only a tiny fraction of the cost of the overall project. Spending a few hundred thousand dollars on a pilot to learn what works (or does not) before investing tens or hundreds of millions of dollars in a project is a form of risk management.

The best pilot projects focus not only on assessing employee satisfaction with the most tangible elements of the workspace strategy but also on exploring underlying social and emotional concerns. Goldman Sachs built their pilot project on a section of the floor in one of the high-rise buildings they occupy in New York City's Financial District. Goldman Sachs, the project's designers, and industry giants Steelcase and Knoll, which supplied the furniture, wanted to know what these financial analysts and sales staff thought about work surfaces, seating, lighting, and fabrics. Did the more open environments work in terms of noise and privacy? Would people use the more informally furnished meeting rooms? They also wanted to know whether the office and workstation sizes were acceptable, particularly to vice presidents who were moving from closed offices to workstations. Issues of this sort go deeper than the functionality of work surfaces and quality of lighting. The company understood that if the workspace design reduced the cost of churn and the total amount of space required, but in the process seriously alienated key segments of its workforce, any real estate savings realized would pale in comparison to lower morale and perhaps loss of talent.

Supporting Work Styles and Assumptions

Although important, the primary deterrent to implementing unfamiliar work practices are not things like the design of desks, storage, or lighting. They are deeply held, and often unstated, values about the social fabric of the office. Employees care about the effect of the new workspace on how status is recognized and on the relationships among staff and between staff and management. These characteristics of the organization are its invisible social infrastructure. Employees' responses to the specific design elements of the workspace are shaped by (1) their sense of how the design meets their expectations and aspirations in relation to such social issues, as well as (2) their own ability to work comfortably and productively and (3) the work itself. Understand and get these right, and the strategy becomes self-generating. Ignoring them is like trying to keep an inflatable boat afloat despite a slow leak: it takes continuous energy, and ultimately the boat sinks.

At Goldman we quickly learned that staff hated the designers' choice of fabrics, which were seen as old-fashioned and incongruent with their image of themselves as fast-trackers at the world's leading financial services company. The ergonomics of the workstations were forcing staff to work in ways they found uncomfortable. The trendy easy chairs in the open meeting areas felt a little unprofessional. The office design conveyed a message of comfort and relaxation, but people preferred a setting that was fast-paced and competitive. Vice presidents didn't like the VP workstation; more to the point, some VPs had workstations and others had offices. Goldman is an extremely competitive environment and occupies an exalted position among financial services companies in part because of it. Employees who made several million dollars a year could still be disgruntled if someone else made more. The flip side was that people would consider accepting a smaller or quite different kind of office or workstation, but only if everyone else got nothing bigger or better. These are social, not technical, issues.

Beyond the Simple Test and Massive Rollout

Most firms invest in a pilot project as a one-time effort to help understand and build familiarity and confidence in what is for them an unfamiliar workspace strategy. The assumption is that once they've learned what works and what doesn't, they can start replicating the new approach across the company. It's an attractive assumption, but it doesn't work.

Key design features that work or don't can be identified relatively quickly in a pilot project. To find out what they are, I like to ask employees about the terms and metaphors they use to describe the new office. At Goldman Sachs employees referred to offices with sliding steel framed doors as "jail cells," to the dismay of the designers who specified them because they looked clean and modern. Very small rooms intended as a place to make a personal telephone call (away from the open plan workstations) were known as "detention" rooms. Employees associated trendy orange colored fabric panels with a 1970s suburban house, that (as one person put it) "my mother would have liked."

In a lot of companies, facilities and real estate managers ignore or play down this kind of employee feedback, since they are under considerable pressure to generate a new workspace strategy that reduces operating costs over time. But they are also held accountable (blamed) if employees are unhappy with the new workspace. The point is not that the pilot design had elements staff disliked. It is that Goldman's commitment to evaluate the pilot identified these design features early on, so they could be eliminated from the final design. This is precisely the purpose of the pilot: to try out design strategies that you are not sure will work.

A subtler challenge arises when assessment of a pilot shows that it works well. Most companies view this as a green light for rolling out the same solution around the company. But leaping from a successful pilot to a corporationwide rollout in one fell swoop is like taking a new road bike out for a successful spin in the neighborhood and then setting off the next day on a trip across America. It takes a while to bring on board the new skills and mind-set needed to handle unpredictable situations and natural variations in the terrain. In the workplace, problems arise because each subsequent project in a rollout pays less attention to helping staff come to terms with new ways of working and the associated changes in attitudes and behavior that are necessary. The extensive time and energy devoted in an initial project to the new design's rationale are lost. Subsequent projects incorporate lessons learned about the physical design (for instance, eliminate sliding steel doors) but abandon the *process* of coming to social and psychological terms with the new way of working, as well as helping staff learn how to work effectively in the new environment.

IBM experienced this in the early 1990s when its UK unit became one of the first large corporations to implement hoteling offices companywide. We assessed these projects around the UK and found continuous technical improvements in design and technology in each new project over time. But these improvements were only weakly connected to employee satisfaction or performance. The most important predictor of employee satisfaction was the nature of the planning process. As the planning process diminished in scope with successive project implementations, so did employee satisfaction. Lost were opportunities for lively discussion and debate of intangible but often more emotionally wrenching issues such as status, supervision, and performance assessment.

In contrast to the sales staff, who were being asked to work in unfamiliar ways, the project planners gained considerable experience and rising confidence in the viability of the new workspace solutions. Given cost pressures at the time, they wanted to just roll out the design solution on a corporate basis as fast as possible. Minimally, they hoped to condense the planning process. They felt the elaborate process used in the first pilot project was no longer necessary. They were right. For themselves. They were also right that not everything done in the first pilots had to be done in every subsequent project. What they had learned about furniture and technology solutions could be applied to each successive project. But for staff in each new project location, the new ways of working still represented a major adjustment. They were being asked to trust a way of working they had not experienced. Rather than being able to air fears and anxieties about promotion, personal and professional identity, performance appraisals, loneliness and isolation, and opportunities for mentoring and professional development, as had occurred in the initial successful pilot projects, staff now were expected to accept the hoteling concept as standard practice.

Failure to continue the kind of process that had worked so well initially resulted in no dramatic failures. Staff didn't quit or openly defy the new strategy. The consequences in such a situation are subtler: lower morale and weaker commitment, and less motivation to overcome small glitches that make the new strategy take root rather than sputter. In the move from initial pilot projects to rollout across the company, some aspects of the original project can be eliminated. Employees' concern that no seats would be available when they came into the office, for example, dissipated over time as experience made clear that this just didn't happen. Other issues, such as the importance of being able to personalize one's own space, or fear that valued social relationships and important face time with supervisors would disappear, are more deeply embedded concerns. Such issues need to be surfaced and discussed with people coming to terms with this kind of new way of working for the first time, even if it has been occurring elsewhere in the firm for some time.

Exploiting Natural Experiments

Formally declared pilot projects occur infrequently, but naturally occurring pilots are an ongoing fact of life in every large organization. As departments are reorganized and relocated within buildings, as leases expire and new leases begin, as new buildings are bought and constructed, space is routinely redesigned. Too few companies exploit these naturally occurring variations in workspace design. New furniture, a change of layout, and new equipment replace the old, without anyone thinking too much about it. These projects don't make headlines. With a standard battery of observational checklists (how spaces are being used, when, by whom, and whether they are the intended uses and users), as well as surveys and interview protocols that ask employees about what works and what doesn't in their new workspace, managers can glean valuable insights quickly and inexpensively (see Chapter Eight). Lessons learned from these naturally occurring experiments can be captured and put on the corporate intranet, where they can feed forward in a continuous learning cycle for each successive project. Once or twice a year the corporate real estate and facility management leadership can come together with key members of business units, human resources, and technology to review them as a whole and explore what they imply for long-term policy and practice. Evaluation and change management merge to become a coherent and consistent form of organizational learning.

Implications for Practice

- If the new workspace strategy is intertwined with major organizational changes that include layoffs, it makes sense to wait until it is clear who will and will not be moving into a new building (for example) before launching a workspace change process. If you are not sure you will have a job or where you will be working, information on office layout and workstations and the like has almost no value.
- Team up with workspace providers in the facility management and real estate units, as well as staff from human resources, to develop a simple but standardized set of tools for assessing the impact of a pilot project.
- Any one method for assessing the benefits and drawbacks of a new workspace pilot project has strengths and weaknesses. So use multiple methods to assess a pilot project: brief Web-based surveys, interviews and focus groups, observational checklists that capture how space is actually used, and photographic documentation of the spaces and its use patterns.
- Culture audits don't need to be long and complicated. Identify a small number of well-informed people, both newcomers and old hands, who can paint a broad but specific picture of the firm and its culture on the basis of their own experience.
- Don't rely on the views of a single person, or even two key people. You know you are beginning to understand what is going on when different people tell you similar things.
- The point of the culture audit is to enter into and shape a project with eyes wide open. Pay attention to what is said, and what isn't.
- Employees at a number of levels in the organizational hierarchy and departments and divisions doing a variety of jobs will have differing concerns. Consider developing information targeted to these audiences so that information is specific and focused, not general and diffuse.

CHAPTER EIGHT

WORKSPACE PLANNING TOOLS

The best management tools don't make decisions; they stimulate informed debate.

For the most part, decisions about workspace depend on tools that bear a remarkable resemblance to those that guided similar decisions when Edison was inventing the light bulb and the Wright brothers started taming the skies. To bring the planning, design, and management of the workspace into the twenty-first century we need to invent new analytical tools. Some may be quite complex, others very simple. The connecting thread is that such tools help managers quickly assess organizational and human resource factors often overlooked by conventional real estate analyses in developing a new workspace strategy—factors that could determine the success of a workspace intervention.

It takes a long time to design and construct a building that can last for fifty or more years. Organizations come and go rapidly, and those that prosper over time constantly reinvent themselves in the face of shifting labor demographics, new technologies, and an enormously complex array of market forces. Finding the right building in the right location with the right amount of space for the right amount of time is a bit like battling weight gain: it's a never-ending process.

What's needed are tools that are conceptually complex. They consider the influence of a range of real estate and organizational factors on building and space requirements and organizational performance—but they must be operationally simple to use. One such early tool, which I developed nearly twenty years ago with Bill Sims, Frank Duffy, and Gerald Davis, was ORBIT-2 (Organizations, Buildings, Information

Technology). Using paper-and-pencil forms and a rudimentary Excel spreadsheet, ORBIT-2 matched an organization's needs for flexibility, technology infrastructure, security, internal communication, and energy against the capacity of selected buildings to support these needs. It was ahead of its time. Real estate and facility management professionals who had spent years developing specialized technical knowledge they applied to complex building judgments were suspicious of such a simple tool.

Today, tools of this kind are valued precisely because they complement rather than replace real estate managers' professional judgment. With them, one can quickly map organizational and building profiles to guide a decision about how much space, of what kind, is needed where and when. Such decision tools enable managers to grasp early in the process where it is most useful to conduct more in-depth analysis, and they give them the sense of what the likely options are along with what it would take to successfully implement them. This chapter is an overview of some of these tools and the critical underlying issues that the tools are meant to address.

Workspace Change and Readiness

Organization leaders pay attention to what their competitors and the firms they admire are doing. Implementing a new workspace design that for another company seems to have reduced costs without undermining customer confidence or employee morale can lead to a poor fit with one's own organization. What's typically overlooked or underestimated is the organization's readiness for change—its interest in and commitment to changing longstanding attitudes and behavior about how space and offices are allocated and designed. Failure to understand the organization's readiness to embrace new ways of working wastes time and money and can significantly undermine employee morale.

Understanding that to propose workspace solutions outside a firm's ability to effectively embrace them invites disaster, one of Japan's largest construction companies asked my firm to develop a simple tool that could help them, early in the consultative process, structure a more effective dialogue with clients about their readiness to change. Collaborating with workplace specialist Alan Drake, we developed a Web-based tool that generates a profile of the organization's readiness to adopt new workspace strategies.

Readiness Tool

The readiness tool draws on judgments of people with extensive knowledge of the firm. Using twenty-five change indicators that are based on extensive experience as well as research on the organizational factors associated with successful workspace change processes, experienced people from various sectors of the company answer questions that yield an organizational profile across six key areas.

Key Organizational Factors Influencing Readiness to Change

- Leadership
- Business Performance
- Operating Environment
- Organizational Culture
- Technological Environment
- Workforce Demographics

Generate a Readiness Profile

Within the six key organizational factors listed in the box, the program asks those completing it to answer a series of questions that in combination characterize the firm along key dimensions (see Figure 8.1). Here are some sample questions:

- The CEO views the need for change as [answers ranging from "unimportant" to "critical"].
- Competitive pressures are ["mild" to "intense"].
- The technology infrastructure is ["obsolete" to "state-of-the-art"].
- The operating environment of the organization is ["predictable" to "unpredictable"].

The tool includes a written rationale for each question (see Figure 8.2), so that those completing the form have a clear sense of not just what the question is, but why it is being asked. Completion of the matrix generates a "readiness profile" in the form of a numerical score that falls within a pre-identified scoring band associated with a specified level of readiness for change (see Figure 8.3). Figure 8.4 describes the organizational characteristics associated with each scoring band.

As suggested in Chapter Seven, such assessments should be part of a cultural audit. Mapping the organization's position on readiness to change using answers to these questions avoids launching an expensive workspace intervention that does not have the necessary organizational support to succeed. It also identifies aspects of the organization that could and need to change if a new workspace strategy is to succeed, so that the organization can make informed choices about whether and where to invest its time, money, and energy.

Figure 8.1. Workplace change readiness tool: sample questions

Factor	Range of response									Scoring		
		Factor rating								Raw	Weight	Total
		1	2	3	4	5	6	7		Score	1 to 3	Score
CEO views need for change as:	unimportant								critical		3	
CEO views workplace as critical to change process	peripheral								central		3	
Mid-level managers view need for change as:	peripheral								central		2	
Leadership style of workplace champion	positional								charismatic		3	
Senior management's interest in workplace issues	very weak								very strong		3	
CEO interest in changing corporate culture	weak								strong		3	
Business Unit leader(s) champion(s) workplace change	weakly								strongly		3	

Factor	Range of response									Scoring		
		Factor rating								Raw Score	Weight 1 to 3	Total Score
		1	2	3	4	5	6	7				
Competitive pressures are:	mild								intense		3	
Cost pressures:	weaker								stronger		2	
Annual cost of churn [moves, changes] is:	low								high		2	
Willingness to invest in infrastructure	weaker								stronger		3	
Operating environment of the organization	predictable								unpredictable		2	
Union presence is:	strong								weak		2	
Condition of the facilites is:	excellent								poor		1	
Organizational change is:	rare								frequent		2	
Culture of organization values risk taking	not at all								very much		3	
Culture values freely sharing information and ideas	not at all								very much		1	
Performance rewarded more than time and effort	seldom								frequently		1	

(continued)

Figure 8.1. (continued)

Factor	Range of response									Scoring		
		Factor rating								Raw	Weight	Total
		1	2	3	4	5	6	7		Score	1 to 3	Score
Employees trust business unit leaders	not at all								very much		2	
Technology infrastructure is:	obsolete								state of the art		3	
Technology competence among staff is:	poor								excellent		2	
Technology support for mobility is:	poor								excellent		2	
Ability to attract/ retain labor	very easy								very difficult		2	
The workforce is primarily:	older								younger		1	
Ratio of old timers to newcomers	higher								lower		1	

Raw score ☐   Weighted score total ☐   Normalized score ☐

Figure 8.2. Workplace change readiness tool factor: leadership rationale sample

Readiness Factor	Low Ready ↔ High Ready
Leadership	

1. CEO views need for change as: unimportant ↔ critical

Most senior executive sets the overall tone for the company. It is very hard to encourage other senior managers as well as staff to change without strong and visible CEO support. The more the CEO views change as critical, the greater the readiness for workplace change.

2. CEO view of workplace in relation peripheral ↔ central
   to change

Workplace-related change will occur more readily if the CEO understands and is interested not just in organizational change generally, but also in how the workplace can contribute to organizational change. The more the CEO views workplace change as critical, the greater the readiness for workplace change.

3. Mid-level managers' view of peripheral ↔ central
   workplace and change

Mid-level managers play a major role in implementing workplace change. Change is more likely when mid-level managers understand how the workplace can contribute to and support their own efforts to increase productivity, reduce costs, and help attract and retain the best-qualified staff. The more mid-level managers view workplace change as central to their ability to meet their own business challenges, the greater the readiness for change.

4. Leadership style of workplace champion positional ↔ charismatic

Change of any sort requires a "champion," someone who enthusiastically and visibly leads the change effort. A "champion" is more than someone occupying a management position (positional authority). Typically, a champion is charismatic; that is, the person is able to energize and emotionally involve others, and is listened to not because of the position they occupy, but by virtue of their personality and way of communicating. The more radical the workplace change, the more important is the role of a charismatic leader. This can occur both at senior management levels for the company as a whole, and/or at the level of the business unit that wants to implement a new workplace strategy.

Figure 8.3. Workplace change readiness tool: sample readiness profile

Factor		Range of response		
		Weighted Scores		
		1 2 3 4 5 6 7 8 9 10 11 12 13 14 15 16 17 18 19 20 21		
CEO views need for change as:	unimportant			critical
CEO views workplace as critical to change process	peripheral			central
Mid-level managers view need for change as:	peripheral			central
Leadership style of workplace champion	positional			charismatic
Senior management's interest in workplace issues	very weak			very strong
CEO interest in changing corporate culture	weak			strong
Business Unit leader(s) champion(s) workplace change	weakly			strongly
Competitive pressures are:	mild			intense
Cost pressures:	weaker			stronger

Range of response

Weighted Scores

Factor		1	2	3	4	5	6	7	8	9	10	11	12	13	14	15	16	17	18	19	20	21	
Annual cost of churn [moves, changes] is:	low																						high
Willingness to invest in infrastructure	weaker																						stronger
Operating environment of the organization	predictable																						unpredictable
Union presence is:	strong																						weak
Condition of the facilites is:	excellent																						poor
Organizational change is:	rare																						frequent
Culture of organization values risk taking	not at all																						very much
Culture values freely sharing information and ideas	not at all																						very much
Performance rewarded more than time and effort	seldom																						frequently

(continued)

Figure 8.3. (continued)

Factor		Weighted Scores		
		1 2 3 4 5 6 7 8 9 10 11 12 13 14 15 16 17 18 19 20 21		
Employees trust business unit leaders	not at all			very much
Technology infrastructure is:	obsolete			state of the art
Technology competence among staff is:	poor			excellent
Technology support for mobility is:	poor			excellent
Ability to attract/retain labor	very easy			very difficult
The workforce is primarily:	older			younger
Ratio of old timers to newcomers	higher			lower

Range of response

Figure 8.4. Workplace change readiness tool: scorecard interpretation

Readiness	Score

LOW   **(<35)**
Companies in this range are not ready for considering a new workplace strategy. They do not have either senior or middle management support. Technology infrastructure of any sort is obsolete or minimal; the willingness to take risks is very low, and the level of trust between staff and management is minimal. Further, while there may be pressures to reduce costs, competition is weak (often typical of government agencies), conservative union presence may be high, and the age of workers tends, overall, to average more than 40 years.

LOW MIDDLE   **(35–50)**
Companies in this range have some, but a limited, readiness for workplace change. They may be willing (in the context of North American offices) to try more open plan office designs, or a universal plan with same-size offices for much of the worker population, but of a smaller size than currently exists. The champions for change more often reside in middle management and in the real estate and facilities management areas than in the business units themselves. However, the way in which people actually work remains mostly unchanged. Technology is adequate for desk-based work, but support for mobile working is minimal. Firms in this range are most often driven by interest in reducing costs, not changing the organizational culture or how work is carried out.

MIDDLE   **(50–65)**
Companies in this range are ready to try some significant changes in the workplace, without them looking like a radical departure from existing practice. Senior management is more engaged and committed to change and to the role of the workplace in facilitating change than in the lower bands. Such changes might include more open plan designs, universal plan and more activity-based approaches, and less use of space to convey status and rank. They are more likely to emphasize flexibility and reduction of costs of churn. While cost reduction is an important driver, interest in supporting more teamwork and collaboration within and across units also plays a stronger role typically. The technology infrastructure is quite good, and management is prepared to spend some money on increasing technology to support mobile work.

LOW HIGH   **(65–80)**
Companies in this range are ready for significant change in the workplace strategy. Management at all levels, including the CEO, are actively and visibly interested in business change generally and understand and are committed to using change in the workplace to further business change. Cost reduction is less of a concern than at lower bands; the perceived need to change the culture and the way work is carried out is high. The technology infrastructure and support for mobile work is high, as are competitive pressures. The workforce tends to be well educated, younger, and more technically competent.

HIGH   **(>80)**
Companies in this range are rare. They are true pioneers and leaders. Their CEO is typically a charismatic leader with a strong, clear vision of how changes in the company's culture and way of doing business can help gain market share, strengthen corporate branding, and help attract and retain staff. Employees are generally well educated and relatively young. Technology is close to state-of-the-art, and management is willing to invest in additional infrastructure if needed. Risk-taking is encouraged, and organizational change is frequent.

Portfolio Toolkit

Organizations are inundated with data. The business challenge is transforming data into useful information that leads to specific recommendations for action, and doing it in a timely fashion. Of critical importance are tools that assess both the need for flexibility to respond to changing organizational requirements and the capacity of the building and portfolio to deliver the right kind of flexibility. Key factors to consider are the frequency with which a business unit is likely to change and require flexibility in its workspace solutions, the adaptability of a facility to respond quickly to changing business needs, and a unit's readiness to adopt alternative workspace strategies such as mobile work patterns and hoteling. Assessing such factors in combination allows quick and pointed discussion with a business unit about optimal sites and future locational planning.

Alan Drake, a workplace strategist with the Bank of America, drawing on the work he did with the author on the Readiness Tool, has developed several additional tools as part of a workspace toolkit that addresses issues of this kind. Like the Readiness Tool, they all share a simple, fast, and transparent methodology. The output is a series of graphs that present data visually, rather than in the more conventional Excel spreadsheet format. In this form, it is much easier to discern overall patterns and the implications for action are clearer.

With all the tools in the toolkit, the common technique is for leaders in the business unit to rate a list of factors that the corporate real estate group has determined are relevant to inform decisions about, for example, the level of flexibility a business unit requires, or an opportunity to employ alternative officing concepts such as hoteling and telework. Each factor is scored and weighted. Weighted scores place the business unit in a well-defined category for which the real estate group has identified in advance the real estate implications (actions to take). Graphing the individual factor scores allows a business leader to see the highs and lows of its overall score and, if necessary, the specific actions that need to be taken to improve a score. Because scores are associated with actions in the tool itself, the data have greater significance for business leaders who more quickly can understand the implications for their own business. This kind of active, graphic visualization of a problem builds business unit interest and commitment in a way that conventional spreadsheet presentations seldom achieve.

The simplicity of the tool generates analyses faster than the bank is accustomed to, which has also contributed to business unit acceptance of the toolkit. The business units had regularly complained that the corporate real estate team took too long to analyze data and make recommendations, thus slowing the business unit's ability to make decisions quickly that allowed it to get on with its work.

Current Real Estate Modeling Approaches

Just as a carpenter's toolkit has more and less sophisticated tools, so too should the toolkit used by those making significant workspace decisions. As we've seen, the Bank of America's toolkit employs simple tools to explore the relationship among real estate and organizational factors. Most existing real estate software focuses on cost issues, in large part because these are easiest to calculate. Few tools are available that simultaneously consider the financial impacts and the human resource factors operating under the conditions of chronic uncertainty that plague every organization today. But competitive position in the marketplace invariably comes not from initial capital and long-term operating costs but from the effect of such real estate decisions on their ability to attract and retain staff, to enable them to work productively and respond to changing market conditions.

A special information technology issue of the *Journal of Corporate Real Estate* captures much of the frustration and inefficiency in the field today.[1] Identified among the factors that account for internal operating inefficiencies making the corporate real estate function "slow, reactive, and bureaucratic" were "inadequate information tools, often consisting of cobbled-together standard packaged software with homegrown or custom applications, each with limited functionality." Tools, increasingly Web-based, exist to help manage space requirements and support asset tracking and reporting; to automate maintenance functions and help regulate energy usage; and to capture and report real estate, employee, and financial information. Yet even the most sophisticated of the corporate real estate tools neglect the human resource consequences of real estate decisions. To develop multifaceted workspace strategies we need to be able to model—in real time—the inherently uncertain human resource factors and financial consequences of possible workspace solutions.

The human resource implications of workspace decisions often lead to solutions other than those based only on the direct real estate costs or space analyses. We've learned the lesson of considering how well something works *in use and over time* in calculating life cycle costs (not just initial purchase price) in making decisions about purchasing such equipment as generators or HVAC systems. We're less advanced when the machine is the office building and the outcome is human performance.

Intuitively we recognize, for example, that if a recommended building consolidation intended to achieve real estate cost savings results in lower productivity, the anticipated real estate savings vanish. Such human resource implications are often talked about but rarely considered in financial models. Firms that are considering building new facilities, undertaking major renovation, or engaged in a merger or acquisition could benefit from modeling the probability that the anticipated benefits will occur.

What is the likelihood that an acquisition will create surplus capacity that can be sold or leased without undermining work processes or negatively affecting attraction and retention? When costs are balanced against the effect on the work process and attraction and retention, as well as the firm's corporate presence in the community, does it make more sense to invest in bringing an older building up to current office standards or in leasing or building new space? Such analyses help clarify the relative costs and benefits of real estate decisions that have major implications for organizational performance. The uncertainty inherent in such human resource and workspace decisions is a fact of life, yet few current workspace models make even a modest attempt to model them.

To stimulate discussion among real estate professionals and organizational leaders about the nature and value of more complex modeling of the interaction of human resource and real estate decisions under conditions of uncertainty, my colleague Art Pearce and I developed a prototype computer model, the Cornell Balanced Real Estate Assessment model (COBRA).[2] The program demonstrates how a single integrated workspace modeling tool can simultaneously consider both conventional real estate factors (construction, operating, finance costs) and key human resource factors (employee turnover, work effectiveness, and so on), and how they might vary in an uncertain business environment.

The Cornell Balanced Real Estate Assessment Model (COBRA)

We started by interviewing senior real estate managers at Fortune 500 and national real estate consulting firms to get a sense of how companies currently were making large-scale real estate decisions. Though hundreds of millions of dollars might be at stake, we found that the typical financial analysis used in evaluating major corporate real estate projects, such as constructing a corporate campus or a significant new building, was a simple discounted cash flow model. It calculates the life cycle present value for the proposed project given assumptions about capital and operating costs and terminal residual value.

The majority of financial modeling programs ignore most, if not all, costs and benefits other than those directly related to real estate. Yet major decisions were often driven by factors such as regional wage scales and the availability of a desired labor force. At Sun Microsystems, for example, a primary reason for selecting Broomfield, Colorado, which is located between Denver and Boulder, for one of its campuses was the availability of an appropriate labor pool and the lower wage scales compared to Silicon Valley in California. Companies routinely take non–real estate factors of this sort into consideration. The problem is that doing so as a separate exercise from financial modeling of other factors makes it difficult to quickly and easily run what-if scenarios to explore the relative effects on the bottom line of changes in other assumptions. How much lower, for example, does turnover have to be in a new site to justify the cost of building a new campus there? What benefits can be realized in terms of communication and collaboration? A single, integrated model makes it possible to test how real estate and human resource factors interact and contribute to a bottom-line cost estimate.

Modeling Core Costs and HR Impacts Together

Using COBRA, or a program like it, managers can consider complex questions: "We need to expand our facilities but we are tightly constrained at our current headquarters campus. To add one million square feet for a new division of thirty-six hundred employees growing to forty-five hundred will cost us $330 million in initial capital costs, including the high cost of underground parking and acquiring an expensive adjacent site. As an alternative, we can build a somewhat simpler facility on less expensive land with surface parking for $200 million four miles away from the headquarters. Is the high cost of co-location justified?"

By loading salary, turnover, and productivity data into the model, the relationship between capital costs and HR benefits can be assessed in a matter of minutes, not hours or days. Core expenses in COBRA include the discounted present value of site acquisition and construction, ongoing operating and maintenance costs, and residual value. Human resource factors reflect the discounted present value of an assumed change in productivity or turnover rate. In this example, the co-located employees would need to be about 5 percent more productive to compensate for the high cost of the co-located facility.[3]

With this kind of analysis in hand, and awareness of relevant research, organizational leaders can make informed decisions, weighing the likelihood of several outcomes. For example, the research we've done assessing the relationship between distance and interaction frequency on a campus (see Chapter Three) suggests in this case that such a significant improvement in productivity (5 percent) is unlikely to occur unless the employees are co-located on the same floor—an impossibility given the size of the employee population to be accommodated.

Modeling HR Implications in Real Estate Projects: Turnover

Turnover represents a major cost for virtually every corporation, and it offers another example of how the new tools can inform decisions. In call centers, where employee turnover ranges from 15–30 percent or higher, a higher level of amenities is often justified on the basis that it would reduce turnover. But what is this relationship? In the absence of hard data on turnover collected in companies that have distinct facilities and amenities, one can either just argue for the value of *some* increased expenditure or make explicit the underlying working assumptions and test their impact. Can project planners and management agree, for example, that it is reasonable to assume a modest 1 percent reduction in turnover with a new building and upgraded amenities? If so, what would be the financial impact of that reduction in turnover? Stated differently, how much extra might it be justified to spend on a facility or amenity plan that management agreed might, conservatively, result in a 1 percent decline in turnover?

Using the COBRA model and a set of explicit assumptions about factors such as salary and turnover costs (which can be changed to test for sensitivity and reasonableness and to reflect the consensus thinking in a particular organization) the relationships among facility or amenity costs and turnover costs can be made explicit. The bottom line in this example is that reducing turnover from 12 percent to 11 percent for an employee population of thirty-six hundred growing at 2 percent per year, with an annual average salary and benefits of $75,000 and a turnover cost equal to 50 percent of salary and benefits, results in a turnover cost savings (NPV) of $13 million over the analysis period of twenty years. The savings can be used to justify substantial capital investment in better amenities.

This same approach can be used to gauge the effect on employees of other types of workspace decision, such as increasing density. What initially (using only the real estate analysis) looks like a clear benefit often disappears in an integrated analysis. We found, doing this kind of analysis, that the $32 million benefit from reducing the number of square feet per person from 220 to 175 was offset by a 1 percent increase in turnover and a 1 percent decline in productivity.

Financial modeling allows organizational leaders to quickly model and test *working* assumptions of this kind. No precise information may exist about the impact of density on productivity, but most analysts can agree about the range of such an impact. Thus, even though some might think the impact larger, all should agree that it would be at least 1 percent. This figure, the model quickly shows, eliminates the presumed value of higher density. The key to such analysis is debating and then agreeing on your company's assumptions.

Modeling Real Estate Implications: Exit Strategies

Most firms considering a corporate campus do so because they have experienced significant, and sometimes explosive, growth over a period of years. Under these conditions, finding any space can be difficult. The solution is often to stitch together a series of quick-fix solutions that result in a patchwork of leased buildings spread out over an area of several miles (as with Sun Microsystems, Apple Computer, and Cisco Systems in Silicon Valley). The alternative, a purpose-built, co-located campus strategy, often looks attractive under such circumstances.

Thinking about an exit strategy at a time when the firm desperately seeks more space can seem a waste of time and energy—or, worse, suggest a lack of faith in the company. Yet, as firms quickly discover when a downturn hits, an exit strategy is of huge importance. A perfect illustration is Union Carbide, occupying a 1.3 million square foot building in Danbury, Connecticut, designed for them without any apparent consideration of how the space could be sublet or sold in parcels if a significant amount of space were no longer necessary. The Bhopal Carbide plant fire in India in the mid-1980s resulted in a tremendous loss of life. Over the long run it triggered major changes in every aspect of the company, including organizational structure and significant downsizing. As a result, for years large portions of the building in Danbury were literally "mothballed," like decommissioned Navy ships, because no tenant could be found for them. The single building, unable to be divided and sold as individual parcels or even easily sublet, simply languished, at considerable cost to the company.

Exit strategy and costs, ignored by some companies during boom periods, have since the 2000–01 economic downturn again become an important consideration. Today, companies seek space that can be readily subdivided (for example, by paying attention to how lobbies, entrances, parking, heating and cooling plant, and commons areas are designed and operated) or marketed and sold to a range of tenants if necessary (say, by establishing each building on the campus as a separate legal parcel). However, no firm that I know of has developed a cost model that simultaneously considers not only initial capital costs but also the ease with which buildings might be sublet or sold depending on their design, their ability to attract and retain staff, or their influence on work effectiveness.

Tools for Managing Uncertainty

As noted in Chapter Six, uncertainty permeates the real estate decision-making process. From projected headcounts that are notoriously inaccurate to unpredictable fluctuation in the costs of construction and borrowing, companies struggle as they decide how much space of a particular type and in what location will be needed, at what point in time, and at what cost. In other fields, risk analyses are an accepted part of any project. No geologist drills for oil without modeling the probability of finding it in a particular location versus the cost of drilling. Environmental risk managers routinely use software programs modeling risk to assess the likelihood that a prospective site has a toxic environmental load against the probable cost of remediation. Real estate professionals use few such models. Typically, analysis compares a best-case, most-likely, and worst-case analysis. But with this type of analysis, it is difficult to get a feel for how uncertain factors interact, and what their overall effect on the bottom line is. Widely available software that uses probability-based, Monte Carlo simulations to model risk and can be easily integrated with standard Excel spreadsheets offers a largely untapped resource for those responsible for planning and managing workspace.

Are Sophisticated Models Needed?

Different tools serve different purposes. Some of the simplest tools we've used, like the readiness tool described earlier, have had a surprisingly large impact. Without doubt, part of their appeal is that it didn't take a huge amount of time or money to develop them. They're also intuitive and thus easily understood and used. Not a lot of training is required.

Tools such as COBRA make more sophisticated analyses readily available, enabling managers to assess difficult real estate and workspace strategies other than on the basis of cost avoidance or savings. But their complexity makes them more time-consuming to learn and apply effectively. The principle behind all workspace planning tools is the same: strip a complex problem to its essentials in order to generate analyses in a reasonable time frame to guide decisions that cannot be pushed back until lengthy studies are completed. Common to both simple and sophisticated tools is acceptance of the fact that one never has all the data one might wish were available. Of necessity, this means making decisions with imperfect information. Yet decisions must be made, and despite the image of tough-minded executives demanding hard data, our experience and research shows that many large-scale strategic real estate–related decisions are based on gut reaction and personal experience.

By making explicit the working assumptions about how the physical environment affects such things as retention and work effectiveness—assumptions that all managers routinely make and use in decision making—one can structure a much livelier and more informed debate than what typically occurs. Minimally, using software models corporate planners and decision makers can quickly test the impact of various assumptions on the financial bottom line. They can compare their assumptions and the basis for them with others so as to sharpen everyone's understanding of the factors that are important and their relative contribution to the costs and benefits of a project. Such tools do not attempt to challenge corporate values and professional experience. But they do furnish a structure that makes corporate values and assumptions more explicit and allows managers to systematically examine how judgments might influence outcomes. Given the stakes, decision makers should welcome such assistance.

Implications for Practice

Use or develop decision-support tools that:

- Are fast and easy to use, but not simple-minded
- Require involvement and input from more than one function in order to stimulate a focused debate about assumptions being made and interpretation of the output generated

- Make working assumptions explicit and create opportunities for them to be debated
- Can be easily adapted as circumstances change and key factors increase or decrease in importance
- Link scores and data analysis to potential actions and strategic direction
- Generate easily understood graphic output
- Vary in their sophistication and complexity

CHAPTER NINE

MEASURING PERFORMANCE

What's important isn't measuring performance; it's changing mind-sets.

For those responsible for planning, designing, and implementing a new workspace strategy, demonstrating the performance benefits of the new design is the Holy Grail. Yet most attempts to do so are remarkably haphazard. Typically, far more time is spent trying to *justify* proposed workspace changes than learning whether or not they achieved their intended objectives. Lots of time and energy are devoted to debating whether it's possible to measure productivity, especially of knowledge workers, and if so then how to do it and which specific metrics make the most sense. This kind of debate misses the larger point. The problem with much performance measurement is its failure to effectively define just what the purpose of the measurement is in the first place, and who the real audience for the findings is.

The ultimate goal should be to change mind-sets about what constitutes the right strategy on the basis of evidence, not assumptions. This demands using a much wider range of potential measurement approaches and performance indicators than what a narrowly defined focus on productivity might suggest.

Defining Organizational Performance

The measurement debate must begin by asking three key questions to test assumptions about what management is looking for in the way of performance assessment:

1. *What, exactly, is meant by organizational performance in the context of workspace strategies and office design?* Don't assume that the most important outcomes are only those formally used to justify the intervention.
2. *What's the best way to assess the value of a workspace intervention?* Don't assume that financial indicators or quantitative data are the only ones that count.
3. *Who wants to know about organizational performance, and why?* Don't assume that all the stakeholders, from project leaders to corporate executives, have discussed—let alone agreed on— what is important to assess and why.

The starting point for any workspace performance assessment is differentiating among three kinds of organizational performance: *facility performance* (efficiency measures involving cost, speed, utilization), *human performance* (behaviors and attitudes believed or demonstrated to contribute to key organizational goals such as speed of delivery or quality of service), and *corporate performance (*outcomes such as number of media mentions in national press and potential client visits that enhance the firm's brand and strengthen its client relationships).

Each measure influences mind-sets and addresses what senior management values differently, using various indicators. The measures used to assess whether the corporate brand has been enhanced differ radically from those needed to test whether operating costs have been reduced. Because most workspace interventions have multiple objectives, with their value typically depending on whom in the organization you ask, it's important to try to structure an assessment program that addresses a range of objectives. In this way the project's real or operative goals will be aligned with what ends up being measured. Failure to do so runs the risk of collecting data that are dismissed as irrelevant.

Facility Performance

From an operations perspective, what's measured is *facility performance:* cost per person, square feet per employee, workstations per employee, construction and operating costs, and so on. In today's dynamic organizations, measures that assess speed to occupy (and exit) space as well as flexibility once in a space are equally important. It's easy to understand why a financial services company that spends $50 million annually on the costs of employee churn in the New York City area alone would want assurances that a new workspace solution will reduce these costs. For other companies, costs can take a back seat to speed, as happened when Monsanto spent as much on a tensile structure as it would have on a comparable building of the same size in order to have a new informatics project team up and running in twenty-eight days rather than months or years. Cost and speed are measures of efficiency: how to do what you do with fewer resources and in less time. They're a valid constellation of valued performance outcomes associated with the facility itself.

Human Performance

Workspace design potentially influences a vast range of attitudes and behaviors. Which ones become part of a performance assessment depends on the nature of the group and organizational goals and objectives, and the specific work processes, products, and services involved. They may also shift over time, as conditions change. At the height of the dot com boom, when the demand for talented computer engineers far exceeded the supply, interest in how workspace strategies affected the firm's ability to attract talent was paramount. In the same organizations three years later, how the design and management of the workspace contributed to teamwork, particularly among mobile and distributed employees, was of far greater interest as organizations looked for ways to maintain national and global operations while containing or minimizing their operating costs.

In the jargon of the manufacturing world, most of these attitudes and behaviors are called "throughputs." They are valued because they contribute to other valued outcomes such as sales volume or market share. Another throughput is teamwork, which depends on effective and timely communication. It in turn depends on trust as well as personal knowledge and experience with other team members. One can probe as many levels down as one cares to. How does the design of the workspace contribute to building trust? Does open plan workspace design significantly increase the likelihood that one will know whom to turn to for advice or feedback in a timely fashion, compared to more traditional closed offices or even shared team rooms? How does the density on an office floor and the layout of workstations influence opportunities for tacit learning and development of a community of practice? Assessing such outcomes produces a contrasting, but complementary, picture of organizational performance from what facility performance does.

Behavioral processes and outcomes of this sort are not unlike those that organizational change professionals routinely consider. What is different is the factors taken into account in trying to understand influences on the likelihood of these desired behaviors occurring. Organizational researchers interested in how much employees retain and apply after attending corporate training programs, for example, focus on factors such as supervisor support and the demographics of the workforce. The organizational ecology perspective incorporates physical factors such as proximity, the layout of workstations, visual sight-lines between employees, and the meaning that employees attribute to design features.

Dig Down: The Five Why's

If you ask a series of questions about desired outcomes, you can follow a chain of answers about the key behaviors and attitudes underpinning these outcomes. These can then be connected to workspace design. For example:

1. What does speed to market depend on? *Decision speed.*
2. What does decision speed depend on? *Flow of information.*
3. What does flow of information depend on? *Trust.*
4. What does trust depend on? *Personal knowledge of coworkers.*
5. How do you get to know your coworkers well? *Interact with them in many situations.*

In this case, the workspace thread connecting all of these desired behaviors to a desired organizational outcome (speed to market) is small-scale groups with minimal physical barriers between individuals, so that visual sight-lines are easily established. They contribute to unscheduled but not necessarily uncontrolled social and work-related interaction that supports behavior that ultimately links to speed to market.

Determining which factors are really important to consider (and gaining consensus about them), as well as taking the time and effort to develop ways to actually measure the factors identified as important, doesn't have to be daunting. The benefit comes from beginning to develop a comprehensive answer to the question of which particular aspects of the investment in a new workspace strategy have added value, and in what ways. With this information in hand, corporate leaders can make informed decisions about where best to invest in either changing the existing environment or rolling out a workspace strategy across the organization as opportunities such as lease expiration and occupancy of new space occur.

Operationalizing Human Performance Metrics

A prestigious global strategic consulting firm initiated a bold workspace experiment, and at the same time devised ways to measure its success. Firm managers suspected that their offices might not be promoting the kind of interaction patterns and learning opportunities that they felt the company needed to maintain its preeminent market position. So they decided to design four floors of a building, each using its own workspace strategy. Some were more open and collaborative, some more closed and focused on concentrative work. Their starting point was asking the question "What is it that makes this company great?"

They identified all sorts of attitudes and behaviors. A strong sense of community was considered critical. Digging down to identify behaviors that contributed to sense of community, they identified such things as knowledge sharing, networking, and social interaction. Getting work done was obviously important, and for that they listed factors such as fast access to necessary resources (human and digital). Each factor then had to be operationalized; that is, they had to figure out what to actually measure. The measurable indicators included communication frequency (number of face-to-face interactions), communication range (number of topics discussed), network diversity (number and type of people outside one's own team), and knowledge of other people's skills and abilities. Once this list was in place, along with the ways these indicators could be measured, the firm developed a research design that would test how the workspace strategies on all the floors influenced these valued organizational behaviors.

Corporate Performance

Facility and human performance measures are integral to most workspace assessment but are by no means the only information managers use to gauge the value of a workspace intervention. Other indicators range from anecdotal evidence and stories that circulate throughout the organization to quantitative data that enhance the brand and promote the company's products and services. Consider the payback on Digital Equipment's Finnish offices.

In the early nineties DEC did a market research survey comparing brand recognition between DEC and IBM. More than 95 percent of the people questioned had heard of IBM and knew it was a computer company. About 8 percent of the people had heard about DEC; most people had no idea what business DEC was in. Pekke Roine, the Finnish country area manager, used a completely unique approach to the interior design of the building to address the branding problem. The design, with its lazy-boy chairs, wall murals, decorative fountains, and swing sets and patio furniture, was so fundamentally different from conventional offices that it generated widespread public interest and brand awareness through media coverage on major TV programs and in leading business journals and newspapers. This media attention brought DEC the kind of brand recognition it sought among the public.

Publicity wasn't the only performance measure used. The genius in the DEC case was that the workspace design contributed positively to all three types of performance measure. The space cost less money, because employees did not have assigned workstations. Employees communicated more with a wider range of their colleagues because they sat in different places and frequently moved around the office. The distinct appearance of the space stimulated widespread and positive media coverage.

Use a Variety of Metrics to Tell the Story

As the DEC examples illustrate, in the best organizations the forms of organizational performance overlap and reinforce each other. Take hoteling, for example (see Chapter Five). At its best, hoteling increases efficiency and flexibility, reduces costs, and helps attract and retain staff seeking an opportunity to work in high-quality space. It can also increase employee satisfaction, widen and deepen social networks, and contribute to a faster and more effective flow of information. If sufficiently unique, hoteling also garners publicity and builds brand identity and recognition. Given the range of organizational outcomes workspace strategies are intended to influence, it isn't surprising that no single performance measure makes the most sense. Certainly, the same measures don't make sense for every organization or even for certain parts of the same organization.

Thus, a balanced scorecard approach to measuring performance, in which a variety of indicators are used to capture the overall impact of a new workspace strategy, is well suited to delineating the diversity of outcomes that organizations value. Ultimately, the goal is to be able to tell an effective story about the company to employees and the marketplace, and to be able to use information about the impact of the workspace on all three forms of performance to make informed decisions about how to invest the company's scarce resources to best advantage.

Choosing Performance Indicators for Assessing the Value of a Workspace Solution

- Select performance metrics that you have some reason to believe are influenced by workspace strategy and design. They won't always be obvious, particularly to people whose training and experience have focused almost exclusively on social and organizational factors.
- Don't blindly copy some other firm's indicators, particularly if that firm is in another industry, market segment, or stage of its evolution.
- Tailor indicators so that they are relevant to and reflect the goals and functions of subgroups within the firm. Employee satisfaction with their workspace may be a measure that makes as much sense for lawyers and marketing as for research analysts and accountants. However, measures of spatial density and cost per square foot of construction vary dramatically, for example, from a trading floor to a call center. One measure won't work for the whole organization.
- Test, don't assume, that the indicators selected actually count with the people in the organization who will make decisions on that basis. Do it by debating and coming

to agreement about which measures make sense with the managers who are asking for and will see the evaluation results. Come to agreement *before* the intervention, not after.

- Link indicators to each other, so that over time one measure can stand in for another. For example, Bank of America is striving to demonstrate that workspace satisfaction affects employee satisfaction; that employee satisfaction affects customer satisfaction; and that customer satisfaction translates into a larger share of the customer's wallet. Once such links have been made, measuring workspace satisfaction by itself becomes a credible performance measure.

Mine Institutional Databases

Generating good data doesn't necessarily require a lot of time or money. Take employee attraction and turnover. The human resource departments of most large organizations regularly track these data. They just need to work with the facility management department to design the database so that the data HR regularly collects can be analyzed by factors such as site, building, and even floor. This makes it possible and easy to explore whether increasing density or changing the layout of workstations has any effect on morale, absenteeism, turnover, and so on. It's hard to interpret such data if they are collected in only one place at one point in time or are presented for the firm as a whole. But if they are collected routinely, it is possible to exploit the kind of natural experiments discussed in Chapter Seven. Over time these small-scale studies make it feasible to identify broad patterns that emerge when observing environment-behavior relationships over several buildings and departments. Differences in management style and philosophy and other potentially mediating factors can be taken into account when the portfolio of a large organization, rather than a single building or a floor of a building, is analyzed.

Financial Data: Numbers Don't Tell the Whole Story

Good managers want some kind of evidence that a proposed workspace strategy adds value. Financial data are important, but they aren't always primary. Nor are they always a straightforward measure. As any econometrist will tell you, you can make numbers generate any outcome you wish. Just change the assumptions.

I saw this a few years ago when I worked with the state of Minnesota on a project. At the time, the state's departments occupied leased space in many buildings of varying quality spread out all over the city of Saint Paul. Senior management wanted a new building constructed near the state capitol. Numbers had surfaced over the years indicating that moving from many leased buildings into a new state-owned building could save tens of millions of dollars over a twenty-year period. My firm was asked to do a financial analysis of some of the alternative real estate propositions. We did.

The analysis showed that no matter how the numbers were tweaked, it always looked as if the choice between a large new building and multiple leased properties was negligible. By the end of a long analytical period, involving many additional financial analyses, the client determined that a new building could be justified. To reach that conclusion, they restructured the project so that an expensive parking garage could be treated as a separate project, thereby reducing the overall projected costs for the office building itself.

Rarely do financial or quantitative data alone justify a major workspace project. A meeting I had with Australian government managers in Canberra illustrates this perfectly. One of the project leaders rather proudly announced that all of their current decisions about building projects were driven only by hard data. No intangible, soft justifications were used. They were hard-nosed about where money would be spent. They used, he said, facility performance measures such as cost per employee, space per person, and energy efficiency, since the government had become interested in sustainable design and was positioning itself as an environmental leader. I had just visited two government buildings that morning, built at the same time and adjacent to each other. One housed the department responsible for immigration and indigenous areas. The other was occupied by the bureau of statistics.

The Australian immigration department's building is a bland, conventional office block. Its materials and furnishings are standard issue. It looks efficient. The Australian bureau of statistics building, less than a block away and built at about the same time, has a much different look and feel. It has a huge atrium with a long, elegant reception counter much like what you'd find in an upscale hotel lobby. Two black leather sofas are the only furniture on the atrium floor. The upper floors house attractive informal break areas with soft furniture and coffee tables. The whole building looks and feels upmarket.

There was no way these two buildings cost the same. When I questioned the government official who had argued that only hard, quantitative data were used in making building decisions, he agreed that the statistics building was more upscale. It had to be, he said, because it housed highly educated and specialized statisticians who were more difficult to attract to government service than was true in the department housing immigration and indigenous areas services. Were there any hard data showing, in advance, that this kind of building would definitely help in attraction or retention? No. Had any attempt been made to track attraction and retention after the move-in?

No. Senior management had sold the need for a different building and fit-out on the basis of an argument about the effects of the building on attraction and retention. It had told stories, not used numbers.

Numbers, whether financial data or otherwise, can and do play a part in decision making. But they are rarely the sole determining factor in justifying a project. The bigger the project, in fact, the less likely are numbers alone to be the driving force. As part of the research we did at Cornell on the value of a corporate campus, we interviewed key real estate managers at a number of leading American organizations. What we heard, again and again, was that decisions involving hundreds of millions of dollars were made on the basis of executive values and beliefs. Sometimes they took the form of a commitment to a city or community ("We've been in this city for a hundred years and are going to stay here"). Sometimes they had to do with comfort level ("There are other Japanese companies in this area, and we want to remain in this area with them"). When CEOs such as Robert Shapiro, formerly at Monsanto, and Paul O'Neill, formerly at Alcoa, abandoned traditional executive offices in favor of open plan designs, they did so for many reasons. Their mind-set about the value of the workspace and how it could foster interaction, teamwork, and collaboration had shifted, over months and years, through a combination of their own experience and insight. It was not a case of hard financial data demonstrating a fail-safe set of benefits.

Measure What Counts

It's worth spending time figuring out what kind of outcomes senior management really cares about before developing any assessment strategy. It may be any or all of the kinds of performance indicators discussed earlier—facility, human, or corporate. There's no point spending time, money, and effort to develop precise behavioral performance measures if the more critical goal is media attention. When one of the Big Four accounting firms developed a specially designed team-based collaborative environment that they believed helped their clients more quickly develop better strategic directions and strategic planning decisions, they had no interest in systematically and formally testing whether this team environment, which they were vigorously marketing as a unique and proprietary consulting tool, actually produced its intended results.

The valued measure was the number of senior executives from potential clients attending the strategy sessions. By participating, these executives gave the consulting firm an opportunity to demonstrate competencies the client might not have appreciated. The value of the highly targeted client interaction was its potential to generate strategic consulting engagements that more conventional meetings lacked. What's measured and how the results are interpreted are shaped within a particular social and organizational context that is neither disinterested nor dispassionate. Data never make decisions; people do. The decisions they make about whether to measure something at all, or what is measured, are the best indicator of what really counts.

Factors Shaping Performance Assessment

The demand for performance metrics (or lack thereof) is shaped by four purposes:

1. *Justifying a new "innovative" program.* Performance metrics can justify doing something that in the absence of clear evidence to the contrary would be rejected on the basis of personal preferences, supposed common sense, and familiar practice.
2. *Preventing a new program from being developed and implemented.* Resistant managers can set the performance level hurdle rate sufficiently high to guarantee failure. In American management culture, where decisions are more easily justified in business terms than from a position of personal power, being able to say "Sorry, but it just doesn't seem to improve productivity, and that is why we're not going to do it" can offer legitimate cover for personal preference.
3. *Protecting individual and corporate reputations.* No program or project is likely to be 100 percent successful. Collecting systematic data can demonstrate the benefits of a workspace intervention; it can also open one up to counterclaims. When any negative, no matter how minor, may be treated as a project failure, little incentive exists on the part of those responsible for the intervention to support a systematic performance assessment.
4. *Continuous improvement.* Learning what works and what does not, and why, characterizes organizations that know they will be faced with continuing workspace decisions and want to benefit from past experience. This approach is what psychologist Robert Sommer called the "Volkswagen" model of evaluation; for thirty years the car changed relatively little in basic form but benefited from literally thousands of small improvements.

The Right Assessment Model

New workspace strategies introduce not just new design elements such as furniture and lighting but new technology such as laptop computers and wireless telephony. Compounding the complexity of the hardware aspect of the intervention, there are often changes in management structure, philosophy, and style. Aspects of the workspace system that one measures at month two are unlikely to be the same as what one measures at month six or eight. Staff come and go, as do managers. The business waxes and wanes with shifts in the marketplace, affecting employee morale and expectations. When Goldman Sachs started to develop a new global workspace strategy in 2000, business was booming—so much so that Goldman Sachs and other major financial services firms in New York City could not find suitable space at just about any price to accommodate their explosive growth. Two years later, the stock market plummeted. Organizational priorities and strategies change.

Summative Versus Formative Assessment

This doesn't mean there's no point in trying to assess the performance of a new workspace strategy. What suits the dynamic nature of organizations is an ecological approach that shifts the focus from a summative to a formative evaluation strategy. The former seeks to assess an intervention at the end of a predefined period of time to judge its success or failure. It assumes that the system being evaluated is the same at the point in time of final measurement as at the time the intervention was initiated. The goal, from an evaluation perspective, is to ensure that the characteristics of the intervention change as little as possible over time. Few organizations exhibit the stability such an approach demands.

Formative evaluation assumes that not only will the organization and intervention evolve over time but that the research itself should contribute to that evolution. It seeks to carefully document how and when characteristics of the system change, and to relate them to observed changes in behavior and other outcomes. When applied to improve conditions continuously, the approach is what academic researchers call "action research." What's learned about how the system functions in relation to program goals is fed back into the intervention to improve its performance over time. In a

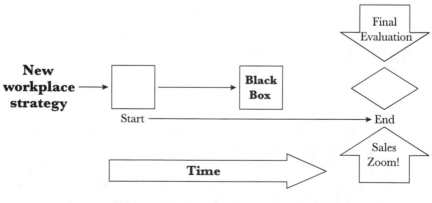

Figure 9.1. Summative evaluation.

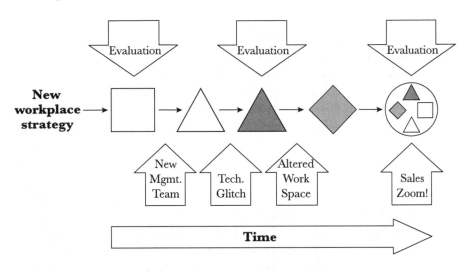

Figure 9.2. Formative evaluation.

Organizational Events over Time

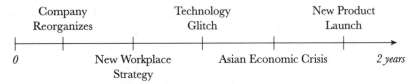

Evaluation over Time

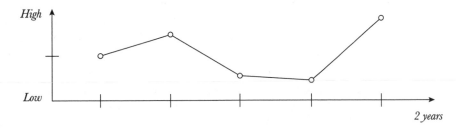

Figure 9.3. Ecosystem assessment.

flexible work program, for instance, if the practice or policy adopted to determine when staff can work at home turns out to dissuade staff from working at home (for example, because it is cumbersome and time-consuming), the protocol is changed to increase opportunities for flexible working, which was the original goal. The original program is not maintained in the face of evidence that it is failing. It is fixed.

The final prize for summative evaluation is a score. For formative evaluation it is insight. The endgame isn't evaluation as a defensive posture, to demonstrate to sceptics that the amount of space and attention paid to a variety of meeting areas or to good-quality ergonomic chairs paid for itself in increased productivity. It's a commitment to understanding whether and why a workspace intervention achieved its desired objectives. As is true of any ecosystem, this measurement approach is characterized by the same kind of messy vitality as the system it evaluates. It uses multiple methods to collect quantitative and qualitative data about what makes the system as a whole work. Management practices and reward and recognition systems are as much in play as lighting, meeting rooms, and workstations. Methods are anything and everything that can throw light on the underlying dynamics of the organization's ecology: employee opinion surveys and interviews that focus on satisfaction with various elements of the workspace system; direct observations about how areas within a building are being used, by whom, when, and in what numbers; institutional data about behavior such as absenteeism, turnover, sick leave, and use of workers' compensation; and tracking of whether more cross-divisional projects and initiatives are launched after co-locating certain divisions.

The outcome of this kind of system evaluation is not precision. It is understanding and insight. Showing that 68 percent of the staff liked or disliked an office tells you that something isn't working. But it doesn't offer clues about what the problem is or how it might be rectified. Being able to explain what staff disliked about that office—and even more so, how it contributed to the way in which they worked—establishes a solid basis for making informed design and policy decisions. Knowing that employees avoided working in highly visible informal meeting areas (as we found in two R&D facilities) because their managers didn't consider time spent in these places as real work imparts a totally new direction for shaping future behavior and allocating resources than would happen if the reason for avoiding these common areas is their poor physical design.

In ecological systems analysis, the focus is on interdependencies. Design influences behavior. Corporate culture influences the design and how it is managed and used. Performance is forged where the values and formal and informal policies, practices, and expectations that make up the corporate culture intersect with the specific nature of the work, the demographic characteristics of employees, all the settings in which work is carried out (inside and outside the office), and technology. From this perspective, measurement is not an event, but a continuous process that knows no departmental boundaries.

At the end of the day, understanding how the planning, design, and management of workspace add value to the business enterprise is a form of fiscal responsibility. It is prudent and sensible, and when done in the spirit of a learning organization it is the headwater for a continuous flow of intelligence that increases the likelihood of scarce organizational resources being used to their full potential. It doesn't have to take forever, nor does it have to cost a fortune. The scarcest and most precious resource is a mind-set that values learning as a key to strengthening long-term competitive advantage.

Implications for Practice: Make It Feasible; Keep It Simple

- Be clear about who makes the decisions. Find out what organizational leaders, the people who will make the decisions, really care about. Are they for, against, or neutral regarding a proposed change? Are they calling for an evaluation and target outcome that they are certain can never be reached? If that is your sense, then the terms of the debate need to be shifted. Don't confuse their concerns with what you think they should care about. Use the differences to spark a debate, and look for ways to incorporate both sets of concerns.
- Secure management buy-in. One of the hallmarks of successful performance assessment is that the underlying methodology, including the kinds of indicators used, is agreed to *before* the study begins. The goal is to avoid key decision makers' criticizing after the fact the data collection methodology (e.g., self-reported performance assessment), the specific measure (e.g., employee satisfaction), the size and type of the employee population (e.g., an unrepresentative sample, for instance), or the time frame of the analysis (e.g., the assessment covered too short a time period) are wrong. The surest sign of decision makers' depth of interest in understanding performance is whether they can find time to actively participate in developing the measurement process itself.
- Determine who (and at which levels of the organization) will get the results of a workspace assessment and how the results will be used. Discuss, in advance, what the implications are for a variety of results. For example, in the early 1990s IBM did employee surveys. Any building whose average rating dropped below 3.5 (on a five-point scale) automatically triggered a closer look at what was causing the low score. Shift the focus from summative to formative research, from final judgement to continuous insight. Make evaluation positive and forward thinking, intended to help shape the future, not to fix blame or protect the status quo.
- Using Web-based surveys, large populations of employees can be continuously surveyed, and the results quickly tabulated. You don't have to interview hundreds of people to get a sense of how something is working. Collect data at least several

months before a move, about three to four weeks after the move, and then about eight to twelve months after that. From then on, collect data once a year or so, to see whether any significant changes have occurred.

- Collect all the relevant facility, human behavior, and corporate performance data you can, both quantitative and qualitative. Use it to weave stories that are relevant and engaging for different audiences, from senior management and staff to Wall Street analysts, the public, and customers.

CHAPTER TEN

MANAGING WORKSPACE CHANGE

*The most effective change agents are the ones who aren't assigned to
the formal change team.*

Managers and staff at most organizations are accustomed to change, at least in
the abstract. Shifts in market strategies, employee benefit plans, even corporate
ownership have become facts of life. But play with an employee's one hundred square
feet of workspace (especially if it's private workspace) and you're playing with fire—
as many scorched managers can attest. Personal workspace is one of the few areas
of business over which employees feel a sense of control. Change it for the worse, and
employees will be reminded of it in tangible, visceral ways every day.

People care about the place where they work because it affects more than their
ability to work productively. It pierces to the heart of their professional and personal
identity, and to their sense of place within the organization (and even within the community). Yet despite the financial stakes and the emotional charge of the issue, and
the number of books, articles, and consultants telling managers how to "manage
change," most companies fail to handle workspace change effectively. Only recently,
in fact, has much attention been paid to managing change in workspace.

The difference between workspace change and other kinds of organizational
change is that employees usually don't have to change their behavior to master a new
compensation plan or organizational structure. Reaping the benefits of new workspace requires a new mind-set; a seemingly simple move from closed to open office
can subvert (in the Alcoa case described in Chapter Seven, deliberately so) the organizational culture. All the unstated (but well-understood) ways of interacting, the
choices about where and when to do the hundreds of mundane things that together

constitute the "job," become less certain. In the open plan, what can I say on the telephone, or in a meeting? If people can see when I am in or out of the office, do I need to spend more time in it to demonstrate my commitment? What can I leave on the desktop? Who will see it? What needs to be confidential? What do I do when I just want to bury my head for a few minutes?

Managers who fail to attend to the cultural change as well as the physical one risk jeopardizing the success of both. The American education establishment discovered the relation between physical environment and organizational philosophy in the 1970s. As a nation we spent millions of dollars trying to create "open education" by building open plan schools. Traditional class*rooms* with doors and full-height walls were replaced with open space areas subdivided by bookcases, tables, storage units, and other furniture to create activity zones for play, reading, art, and other activities. We built them, but we didn't spend much time or effort helping either teachers or students develop the skills needed to teach or learn effectively in them. Teachers repositioned bookshelves and magazine racks and supply cabinets to re-create, as best they could, the older conventional classrooms with which they were familiar. In these spaces they knew how to act right, how to be civilized.

Companies spend tens of millions of dollars on renovation and much more than that on new buildings. They do it to accommodate growth in the number of staff and new technologies, enhance communication and collaboration, change their image, lower their occupancy and operational costs, attract and retain staff, be nearer to customers or suppliers, and create more flexible and dynamic facilities. But if staff don't take advantage of and are not committed to the new workspace, the company might as well just throw hundred dollar bills out the window while chanting the secret corporate mantra. An effective workspace strategy requires that people understand and accept the new ways of working implied in the new physical facilities, and *that* requires something lots of firms, and the managers who guide them, find difficult: being clear and honest about the factors driving the change.

Drivers of Change

High on the list of factors driving change in the workspace is reducing cost. In the face of fierce global competition, large executive offices, or even small field sales workstations occupied a fraction of the time, waste scarce corporate resources. This is the economic logic behind hoteling, and any company contemplating such a move should be straightforward about it.

A second model for workspace change, activity-based design, addresses another reality. Analysis of how people actually work reveals that few people do more than one or two activities at the same time. People don't talk on the telephone, write a report, and meet with someone else simultaneously. Yet workstations and offices have been designed over the past fifty years or more as though all the work of the day does—and should—occur in the same place. No longer. Companies are now more willing to consider workspace as a system of loosely coupled settings: a small workstation, perhaps like a library carrel or self-contained mobile desk, is linked to an informal break area, library, conference room, or other specialized work settings by the physical movement of the worker and the electronic transfer of information. It's a significant mind-shift that reflects how people are actually working, and it promotes a more efficient use of space. Corporate efficiency by itself won't motivate employees.

The functional drivers and enablers for workspace change, such as reducing cost and improving communication and teamwork, are easy to understand. But when the solutions for achieving these goals—say, smaller, more open offices or being mobile within and outside the office—are seen as a threat to expression of status or undermining our professional competence, identity, and prerogatives, we fight back.

Managing workspace change is all about creating and implementing a process that helps employees believe the workspace change is in fact beneficial not just to the company but to them personally. The research we've done through the International Workplace Studies Program at Cornell over the past fifteen years as well as experience helping organizations implement new workspace strategies point to some clear lessons about what kind of change management activities works, and what kind does not.[1]

Making the Case for Change

Helping employees embrace changes in how, where, and when they work isn't rocket science. It's harder than that, precisely because there are no definitive solutions. New technology, by contrast, is precise. When it works, it works. When it doesn't, it's hell. Getting technology right can be expensive, but the fixes are fairly obvious. Push the right button, and presto! the screen reappears. Human emotions are more volatile. There is no big button you can push to prevent damaged egos, hurt feelings, a sense of abandonment, resentment, apathy, and other human emotions from exploding.

It's not obvious how we can best help an enormously diverse group of people, differing in age, gender, experience, race, education, income, life cycle, and lifestyle, let alone personality, embrace new ways of working. We don't know all the answers, in large part because as with any complex ecological system the combination of factors and how they relate to each other are never precisely identical. But we have learned, even if not precisely, that there are better and worse ways to manage workspace change.

Avoid Four Common Mistakes

1. Don't rely on formal presentations and written materials.
2. Don't assume that since you've told them already, you don't need to tell them again.

3. Don't assume that change management starts with move-in and stops after it. It begins when the project begins and continues after occupancy.
4. Don't focus on the physical design and technology and short-circuit the cultural issues. Involving staff in the design process is not the same as involving them in a long-term culture change process.

Beyond Scripted Efforts

Focus groups, employee surveys, building information days, special newsletters, employee hotlines, and other planned change activities don't just pop up. These activities require resources, and lots of them. Staff are needed to design and implement the activities and events. Employees who participate in and take advantage of change programs take time from their so-called real work. In balancing these costs against the fact that in most organizations today few people are going to quit their job because they don't happen to like a new workspace strategy involving smaller or unassigned offices, or working more in teams, why bother with all the time and effort of a planned change strategy?

The answer lies in the fact that because people don't quit doesn't mean there are no negative consequences. Speed and quality aren't enhanced by employees spending hours complaining about the new workspace strategy with colleagues. A thousand employees painting a negative picture of the company to family, friends, and professional acquaintances they meet outside the company doesn't make attracting the best talent available easier. Ten percent of the employee population making less than a total effort to make the new strategy work when glitches occur and gravitating to their old way of working whenever possible undermines the time, money, and effort spent to develop and implement the new strategy.

None of these behaviors *in itself* makes a huge difference. But cumulatively, multiplied across hundreds or thousands of employees, behavior shapes the organization's character. Airlines cut back on complimentary peanuts that cost only a few pennies per passenger because over millions of passengers they show up on the balance sheet. The cost saving is obvious, but the long-term effects on corporate loyalty, influencing whether a disgruntled passenger will fly the same airline again if other options exist or recommend it to someone else, are much less clear though potentially far more consequential. The question isn't whether to mount a planned change process or not. Employees need to understand what the change will be, why it is occurring, and how it will affect them personally. The key question is how to get value for money. How can change be managed so that whatever time and money is spent actually reduces resistance and increases commitment to the new strategy?

Understanding the Work Process

Involving staff in helping shape the details of the new workspace strategy itself is the first, and most critical, step. It may be framed as part of the design process, but in reality it marks the beginning of the change process. Engaging staff increases the likelihood that the final design will enable employees to work productively. You wouldn't pay $30,000 for a car that doesn't always start on a damp morning. Why pay hundreds of thousands of dollars for a workspace that supports productive work patterns only some of the time? Buying a filing system that employees find useless or installing workstation modules that make it difficult for sales staff to build and maintain good customer relationships throws money down the drain. Value for money comes from investing in a design process as well as physical design that actually makes a difference in how employees are able to work and how they feel about the company.

The experience of a major telecommunications firm that spent hundreds of thousands of dollars redesigning its telephone sales center without understanding the underlying psychology of call center operators illustrates the point. Hundreds of staff sat at desks in an open area making sales calls. Try it some time. The stress can be acute. Not all customers appreciate unsolicited attention, particularly around dinner time. Not infrequently, customers explained this to the sales staff in language that would make a sailor blush. To blow off steam and vent frustration between calls, staff often chatted for a few seconds. Wanting to boost sales, the company saw this social behavior as wasted time. To boost productivity the space was redesigned with high-paneled cubicles that separated the telephone sales staff from each other and prevented visual contact. The intent was to boost productivity by reducing what management saw as idle chatter.

It backfired. Staff's idle chatter was, in fact, a significant release valve from stressful and frustrating phone calls. Sales plummeted rather than increased, until the firm went back and removed the panels and created an environment in which the staff could see and talk with one another. Good intentions really can pave the road to hell. The answer is not just to ask staff, "How should we redesign your physical environment?" They may not know, especially in advance of experiencing a new design.

Understanding the work process requires more than paying attention to just surface-level functionality (a staff person needs a telephone or computer to make a call or develop a spreadsheet). The social and psychological aspects of the work are, as the telecommunications firm discovered, a facet of functionality. For sales and support staff, the social aspects of work are not incidental. They are what often make a boring job tolerable. For secretaries it may be the opportunity to associate with higher-ranking managers and having a privileged window on what is happening in the firm. For an engineer the most rewarding aspect of the job may be the opportunity to be part of a cutting-edge entity where you can associate with the brightest and most innovative minds in your field. Create a design that reduces social relationships, and you have chipped away not just at comfort or convenience but at the foundation of what makes the organization as a whole tick.

Staff need to be consulted, with the focus not on solutions they prefer but on how and why they work the way they do and what makes them and their team productive and engaged. I recently ran a workshop for a team of people who were going to move from the organization's headquarters to a satellite office about three miles away. Before the meeting even started, the head of one of the departments involved in the move pulled me aside to let me know that, whatever else might be decided, the nature of her work required a "proper" office, not a workstation. She was disappointed and suspicious when I said "Thanks" but told her we were not going to start by focusing on solutions. At the end of the workshop she volunteered that she hadn't realized there were so many ways of thinking about open plan offices, and that given how the new team wanted to work she was now more open to considering something besides the closed office she initially thought was the only possible solution.

Engaging Employees in the Process

Task-oriented managers' initial response to most staff engagement processes is that they're a waste of time ("I hired these people to design computers. We're paying the architects to design the building. Let's get on with it!"). Done right, staff involvement not only generates better design solutions (because they are grounded in a deeper understanding of work processes) but has the potential to become a form of organizational glue. By "done right" I mean consciously and deliberately developing the design process in a way that helps identify and clarify organizational goals, reinforces the culture's values, strengthens and improves the social bonds and trust between staff and with management, and motivates everyone.

This goes beyond the usual "capacity programming," which calculates things such as how much space is needed to accommodate a desk, a computer, or a person getting into and out of a chair. Getting these physical, or human factor and ergonomic, conditions right is not a trivial task. Getting them wrong can have significant implications for a company forced to cope with the costs of everything from wasted effort to carpal tunnel syndrome. Capacity is the beginning, not the end point, of an effective design process. It's necessary but not sufficient.

Once a cultural audit has been completed and there is a good sense of the barriers and opportunities for change, the process for planning and designing the organizational ecology of the workplace can play a more subtle and larger role. Encouraging employees to discuss how they work, how they can work smarter, and how their work links to the organization's strategic intent is invaluable in its own right. It clarifies how their individual activity fits into the whole, and it focuses attention on what the organization, as well as the individual, really needs to do to be competitive.

The opportunity to discuss such issues communicates a level of management commitment and sensitivity to staff that most organizations constantly struggle to achieve, often with only limited success and greater cost, through more conventional human resource and organizational development programs.

Avoiding Managerial Pitfalls

The temptation to skimp on necessary resources or shortcut the design process can be fatal to a change effort. A large insurance firm I worked with decided teamwork was its long-term key to success. Naturally, they wanted an environment that supported and enhanced collaboration. Like a lot of companies, they identified a few other organizations with similar goals and arranged for site visits to see what they had done. They visited the R&D laboratories of a leading consumer products company and the team areas for executives at a leading contract furniture company.

These are the right things to do, if at the same time that you are seeking insight and inspiration from the physical designs of others you also gain understanding of what it took for those companies to move from where they were to where they are at the moment. It's critical to explore the differences as well as similarities in the nature of work processes, organizational goals and aspirations, corporate culture, and leadership. Unfortunately, this particular insurance company wanted to innovate, but it also wanted to maintain the same kind of project schedule that had worked for them in the past. They expanded by building a new wing that was a dead ringer for the existing one.

The result was totally predictable: frustration, disappointment, resistance, and apathy instead of the cooperation and enthusiasm essential to genuine and sustained innovation. Benchmarking as imitation is like visiting a master cabinetmaker, taking note of what tools are in the workshop, and then buying the tools while expecting to build a finely wrought piece of furniture. You could outfit my garage with the world's best carpentry tools, but I can assure you that you would never want to put what I built in your house. What's obviously missing is the time, experience, and skill needed to get the most out of the tools.

Also missing from most workspace change efforts is an appreciation of the gestation period for innovation. By the time a new workspace strategy is implemented it's not unusual for the *concept* of a new way of working to have been gestating for years inside that company (and the marketplace generally). Ideas often start in small firms, or in small corners of large firms, spreading slowly from firm to firm and department to department. Initially the field may be fallow, the conditions inhospitable. Senior management may be too comfortable with past success, or too close to retirement to expend the energy needed to challenge themselves and the culture they helped create. Economic conditions may not generate sufficient fear or incentive to change. But all the while, the ideas are percolating, close to or just beneath the surface.

For instance, images and the stories about innovative offices circulated widely in work-place conferences and forums around the world in the late 1980s and early 1990s. People like Lisa Joronen, the head of SOL, a corporate cleaning firm in Finland, spoke at major real estate conferences in the United States. She described her own efforts to turn inside out the concept of how an office should look and function by creating an office with roots more in a comfortable home than a factory. Researchers and consultants who had visited and studied such firms as SOL, DEC Finland, and IBM in the United Kingdom came back to the United States and, through talks at professional societies, in publications, and consulting engagements, gradually enriched the image bank of U.S. architects, designers, and facility managers and corporate real estate professionals. Initially, many of us came home from these site visits or conferences with our mouths slightly agape, not quite sure we had really observed such radically different approaches to office design. But over time these concepts began to take hold in companies that just a few years earlier would not have dreamed of offices where employees had no assigned workspace and the company provided a budget for staff to purchase furniture and equipment for a shared commons areas that lacked the uniformity many companies associated with being professional and projecting a strong corporate image.

This team-oriented cluster makes it easy to observe nonverbal cues about whether someone is busy or open for conversation. The result is fewer un-wanted interruptions than in an office cubicle.

Realizing that what you observe in another firm and might want to immediately implement in your own may have slowly taken hold and become acceptable in that firm over months or years of conversation is an element of workspace change management that's widely overlooked. This informal, below-the-radar learning process contributes to readiness to consider workspace options that without this gestation process would be summarily dismissed.

The Sociology of Change Management

The unfortunate truth about much of change management is that it comes too late in the process and is driven by the need to cool off workers angry and disappointed with a new environment that they had little opportunity to meaningfully influence. Justification for the new space too often patently misleads and masks the real reasons for change, which management fears the workers don't value and will resist. Such change efforts, to the extent they are intended to reduce resistance and speed adjustment to the change, fail. Employees don't resign en masse or riot. More often, they just withdraw a little more of their energy, commitment, and motivation.

This is not to say that even effective change programs render everyone joyful and enthusiastic. Hardly. Not everyone loves the current work environment; nor will everyone love the new one. One of the toughest challenges for management is to separate resistance to change grounded in serious deficiencies in the proposed or new environment (deficiencies that undermine productive and satisfying work for employees) from resistance grounded in an unwillingness to consider making an effort to learn new skills, manage relationships differently, or work in new settings.

Individuals and organizations seek to maximize their self-interest; to develop a sustainable enterprise that prospers over time both must compromise. Yet when I've asked managers planning a workspace change the simple question, "What incentive is there for your people to embrace the proposed change?" too often the answer is puzzled silence. It is as though the incentives are self-evident to everyone. Trust me, they're not.

If you are a real estate or facilities manager and you reduce the company's workspace by 30 percent, management will recognize and reward you for your efforts. But what about the folks who are now sitting in tiny workstations, working from unassigned offices, and using smaller break rooms? What's their incentive for getting on board? By "getting on board" I mean being committed to the change, interested in making it work once the inevitable glitches surface, and willing to help persuade skeptical colleagues that the change is worth supporting.

Change that is good for the organization may not be good for all employees, and vice versa. But good change programs reflect a deep understanding of what is needed to keep the best people on board, working in a way the firm's leaders believe is required to prosper going forward. This means understanding how the design, allocation, use, and management of space and time interact to produce desired attitudes and behaviors.

Confronting the Action Trap

Engaging staff takes time. Yet for many American managers "managing" means taking action *now* ("Stop talking and do something"). Talking with staff is viewed with suspicion because it is open-ended, ambiguous, time-consuming, and not infrequently filled with emotions. When contrasted with a view of action as hard, fast, unambiguous, and exciting (you can see when a wall goes up, but not when a psychological barrier comes down), it's easy to see why managers are often suspicious about employee involvement.

The dilemma for managers is that fast action can ultimately slow or derail a project or program. Yet extensive consultative processes by themselves are no guarantee of good decisions or positive outcomes. Take Lloyds of London, the venerable London association of insurers. In 1987 it moved into what was at that time the most expensive new office building in Europe, designed by the Richard Rogers Partnership and located at 1 Lime Street in the City of London. Considerable effort had been made by the planning team to understand how the insurance market worked and the role information technology was and would continue to play in transforming it. Good intentions were not in short supply, nor were world-renowned architects and dedicated and bright project managers. Yet about one year after initial occupancy, the property manager for Lloyds estimated that some $50 million would be needed to renovate the building to work optimally. Many of the problems had been recognized earlier, through staff involvement. But recognizing something and heeding its implications are not the same thing. Jeffrey Pfeffer and Robert Sutton call this the "knowing-doing gap."[2]

An action orientation can lead to quick initial decisions that often come under attack at a later point because not everyone involved understands or agrees with them. Unforeseen issues arise that in a more effective process are likely to be uncovered and resolved early on. The practical consequence of short-circuiting the planning process in its early stages is that time and money, as well as enthusiasm and energy, are lost as a project grinds to a halt for reevaluation, retooling, or in severe cases abandonment. For those concerned with demonstrating that they are adding value to an organization one thing is certain: getting a project done on time and within budget *that fails to meet its diverse objectives at a high level* is not adding value. Paying attention to process issues may take more time initially, but ultimately it improves the quality and speed of the overall project.

The Power of Informal Change Agents

One of the most surprising findings to come out of our IWSP research was that despite virtually every organization studied believing it had created significant opportunities for employee involvement in the change effort, more than 80 percent of the employees in these companies did not feel they had been involved.[3] Companies held town hall meetings in which the goals and nature of the new workspace strategy were explained and questions answered. They created special project hotlines and newsletters that addressed issues the staff had raised in interviews and focus groups. None of it made much of an impression on employees. Change processes that result in employees feeling involved are critical given the strong relationship between perceived involvement and a positive response to a new workspace strategy. We found that employees who felt involved were much more satisfied and committed to the change intervention, more likely to try to make it work, and less likely to want to revert to the previous workspace solutions.

In trying to make sense of this gap between intent and reality, we realized that the people setting up and participating in formal events such as town hall meetings, focus groups, and office tours feel involved, as they should. But only a small percentage of the total workforce affected by a workspace change participates in an event of this kind. The widespread reliance on formal change management activities is not likely to have much positive effect on employees generally. The opportunity to attend a town hall meeting in which senior executives and project leaders talk about the project and invite questions helps get the word out about the project, but there aren't a lot of rank-and-file employees who are going to stand up in a public meeting and challenge the CEO by asking hard questions or observing that "You've said that before, and nothing came of it!"

Both data and experience suggest that what counts as employee involvement is some form of personal interaction. A survey might go out to all members of staff, but it is impersonal and offers no opportunities for dialogue or interchange. Planned change activities such as town hall meetings and special project newsletters don't count experientially because most people consider only face-to-face communication as the real thing. This kind of personal interaction has to occur more than once, and not necessarily in a planned way. Because in projects with more than about fifty people the feasibility of involving everyone directly is low, the paradoxical key to the riddle is to formally plan for informal communication.

Cascading Information Flow

An informal and continuous face-to-face information flow helps avoid the sense that the real reasons for the workspace change, as well as its finer details, are being withheld. Personal interaction draws key opinion leaders throughout the organization into the informal change process. These dispersed leaders are the people in a department or team that others come to know and trust. They can be identified by asking people whom they go to when they want to know what's going on in the organization or are seeking particular expertise. Some of these opinion leaders ultimately may become champions of change. (Every significant workspace change program I've seen had a champion—someone, at whatever level, with the passion, vision, energy, credibility, and enthusiasm to attract others.) But not all of the informal leaders will be advocates for the new workspace strategy. They don't have to be. The intent is to create a cadre of well-informed informal change agents prepared to answer questions with accurate information.

Informal Change Agents

- Make a conscious effort to identify opinion leaders within the organization, at every level.
- These informal opinion leaders (they may not occupy any management position) are a rich source of potential informal change agents. Give them the resources (for example, accurate information about the change, presented in a simple and accessible form that can easily be shared and discussed with others) and encouragement to play a positive role in the change process.
- Don't pressure the informal change agents to be uniformly positive. Ask them only to furnish accurate information and an open mind.
- Other informal change agents, often unrecognized, are family, friends, and professional peers in other organizations. Incorporate family into the change process (invite them on site visits; offer information intended to be taken home and shared with family members, including children) as well as professional peers (place information about the project in trade newsletters and journals in a positive light).

For this kind of cascading information to flow freely, opinion leaders need information at their fingertips about project goals and time lines; how work processes of specific individuals, teams, and departments are affected; and realistic schedules. Members of the core project team can explain and distribute this information to group managers and opinion leaders, people esteemed for their expertise, judgment, and experience. How information is transferred can take any number of forms, from simple one-page diagrams that serve as a talking point to a short animated Web-based tutorial.

Being prepared to answer employee questions and concerns whenever they surface, not three weeks or several months down the line when the next formal change meeting or event is scheduled, is the critical success factor. As new information about the project surfaces or is needed, the process begins again at the top, cascading down. Unlike nature's waterfalls, information, concerns, and ideas can also flow upward in this process. Individuals or groups raising questions or issues can pump information back up the informal change network. What's different in this model is the reliance on a small, core team to start an information flow, rather than being responsible for controlling and disseminating all information in a highly prescribed manner.

The second factor that enhances employees' sense of involvement is the opportunity to contribute to the outcome. Most of us want more than to voice our opinions (particularly on an impersonal survey). We want to feel that our opinions and views make a difference and that we influence decisions. Even better, we want to make some decisions ourselves. Ultimately, the only way to achieve real decision making on a broad scale is to build into a workspace intervention the opportunity for every individual to directly influence or decide something about how he works and his work environment.

How to Involve Employees

- Surveys don't count as involvement for employees. Create opportunities to review floor plans, furniture, workstations, and colors as early as possible.
- In a large organization it isn't feasible to have every employee directly involved in nitty-gritty decisions about design choices. Form project teams or task forces to make recommendations, and make sure they represent a true cross-section of the firm. Have groups nominate the people they want to participate so that they feel their viewpoint is being represented.
- Be clear about where you are prepared to accept employee recommendations, and where not. Project leaders should not confuse in their own minds (or employees') input with decision. All input and no recommendations is unlikely to generate much enthusiasm or commitment.
- One good way to combine some overall control about decisions for furniture and colors is for the project leaders and designers to develop a preapproved range of choices, all of which are acceptable. Within that menu of choices, what the employee groups select is included.
- Give employees information about which decisions their feedback has influenced (be specific), and where their feedback was heard but did not change an initial decision (and explain why).
- Create opportunity for meaningful decisions (not just input) at every level of the organization, from division and department to team and individual. This may include decisions about how to lay out furniture and equipment within an individual or team space, decisions about colors for a floor, and so on.

This doesn't mean that every employee is going to decide on the building's location or architectural design. It does mean that there should be opportunities for the employee to decide at least a few elements within the workstation (with freestanding furniture, such things as how it is laid out, or whether she wants more file cabinets or bookshelves). At an absolute minimum, employees should be able to adjust things such as lighting and seating. Opportunities for group choice are also important. Drawing on my experience in Sweden, I proposed group-defined areas for Apple Computer's new R&D campus. Rather than the architects and designers deciding every last detail of design, the group occupying a portion of a floor could elect how it wanted to use and furnish the space and was given a budget to purchase furniture or equipment for its common areas. The visual consequence of such an approach is that the commons areas dotted around the floor are distinct. Some have sofas and easy chairs or a picnic table and brightly colored umbrella; others feature work tables and layout space.

Group choices of this kind are small but meaningful. They affect the everyday quality of one's work life and are valued for that reason. The organizational benefit of this evident diversity is employee commitment and motivation, a sense of being valued and recognized as more than an anonymous cog in a corporate wheel. Everyone, and every group, feels unique. Recognizing this basic human need doesn't have to undermine a strong sense of corporate branding, or tasteful and even sophisticated design. Think of expensive row houses in New York, Chicago, or London. Gardens, lighting, furniture, and design details give these streets wonderful character without undermining the strong overall design concept of the buildings themselves. The variation enhances the whole, rather than detracting from it.

In inviting employee involvement it's important to remember that people often expect managers or staff who ask for their views to make available whatever they request. Setting the financial and design boundaries of a project is imperative in this regard. Employees need to know why a suggestion has been rejected. In the hospital project described in Chapter Six, we understood and agreed that redesigning the basic layout of this older facility would directly contribute to nurses' efficient use of time. But it is hard to do major reconstruction on a $5,000 budget. Part of setting the boundaries was indicating to staff that we wanted to know what the perceived problems were, and that we would then look for ways to solve them *within our very limited budget*. We wanted to encourage people to discuss what was wrong without imagining an expensive solution to the problem. In the end, simple, inexpensive solutions improved both patient and staff satisfaction with the environment and their views about the quality of health provided.

Why Employee Engagement Matters

The benefits of meaningful staff engagement, as Figure 10.1 shows, are clear. They include a stronger commitment to the new workspace strategy; more satisfaction with it; and less interest in returning to the previous, more conventional workspace.

Counterintuitively, it makes the job of management easier. The pressure to be the only idea person dissipates. The numbing, exhausting work of monitoring and controlling gives way to the pleasure of praising and extolling. It's a lot more rewarding.

From a management perspective, getting employee engagement right means being committed to sharing control (not giving it up), being honest (about which decisions staff can affect and which they cannot), accepting diversity (your staff may make good decisions that are different from those you would make), and exerting leadership rather than power. It's not easy, but it is a way of unleashing the stored energy and intelligence of the organization's most expensive resource: its staff and management.

So why, given all we've learned about change processes over the past sixty years, do we still so often find resistance to change? The answer is that most workspace change, at least initially, threatens familiar and comfortable work patterns and disrupts valued social relationships.

In the end, we embrace change that we can imagine enhancing our sense of personal and professional identity. This reinforces, strengthens, and expands valued personal relationships and competencies. Short of that, we may accept change with resignation, as something necessary but not welcomed. Or we may simply resist (usually below the corporate radar) new working practices. Good change management achieves, minimally, acceptance of if not enthusiasm for a new way of working. But it cannot do so without being embedded in and integrated with the nature of the workspace strategy itself, and the process for its design.

Figure 10.1. Benefits of feeling involved in the change process.

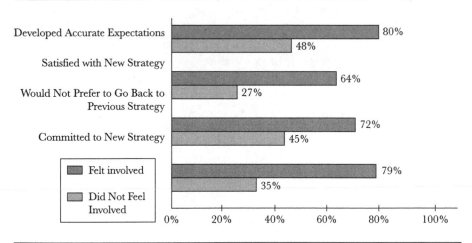

Source: Becker, F., Tennessen, C., and Dahl, L. *Managing Workplace Change.* Ithaca, N.Y.: International Workplace Studies Program, Cornell University, 1997.

Implications for Practice

- For employees, the most critical factor in a workspace change is the opportunity to give voice to their concerns, desires, and expectations to the firm's leaders and their own managers. Supplement companywide broadcasting of initial news about a major workspace change or intervention with small face-to-face meetings between supervisors and their direct reports.
- Communicate the reasons for change that are truly driving it. Don't be afraid to talk about issues that at least some employees won't agree with. They will identify the issues in any case, and then conclude that the truth was being withheld and become even more resistant.
- Communicate realistic expectations, including what some employees may consider negative outcomes, about the consequences of the change for individuals, teams, and departments.
- Don't ask for employee input or feedback on decisions that have already been taken.
- Understand that venting anger or disappointment upon initially hearing of change is normal and expected; don't overreact to it. Listening is the greatest asset at that point.
- Employees often do not understand the overall project process, from conception through design and implementation, and where they fit into that process. They may expect information regarding the impact of the change on them sooner than the project planners and designers themselves know. Without understanding the overall stages of the project, employees may incorrectly assume information is being withheld, when in fact it is not.
- The change experience can be a major stressor for employees. Recognize the stages of coping with change. Be prepared for denial, anger, low morale, and reduced productivity for three to six months.
- Distinguish between employees who resist change on the basis of personal preferences or values (difficult to overcome) and those who identify facets of a new workspace strategy that can be demonstrated to be dysfunctional and annoying (more readily fixed).

CHAPTER ELEVEN

THE VALUE OF UNCOMMON SENSE

Common sense feels right; uncommon sense can work right.

Iwork with many organizations, both as a researcher and consultant. I cannot think of any that are not faced with what, in the Introduction, I called organizational dilemmas (Horst Riddle's "wicked problems"). As earlier chapters indicate, they range from questions of physical layout and location that promote development of knowledge networks and cross-functional collaboration to questions of measuring the performance of workspace strategies and effectively managing workspace change.

Much of my consulting revolves around clarifying the pros and cons of approaches to addressing issues that have no simple solution. What I find time and again is that decision makers fall back on familiar solutions, tried but not necessarily tested. That's understandable. Under great pressure of cost and time, we rely on what's worked before. We're less likely to make major mistakes that way. But we're also unlikely to make a valuable breakthrough. It's a safe but not necessarily effective strategy for improving organizational performance.

On the other hand, to bet the house on a single new or unfamiliar approach makes no more sense. As discussed in Chapters Six and Seven, this is the point of developing multiple workspace strategies that advance both conventional and novel strategies at the same time. Experience with alternative workspace solutions, policies, and practices that can be implemented quickly at some point in the future, because of past experience with them, become a knowledge option. Seventy-five percent of the workspace portfolio may be in conventional class A office buildings. Experimenting with prefabricated, tensile, mobile, and other construction approaches for the other 25 percent solves immediate problems and builds confidence born in experience as to what works best for one's own firm.

Understanding the Full Range of Risks

In the face of chronic uncertainty affecting every facet of the business enterprise, organizational leaders need to understand their (as well as the corporation's) appetite for risk. What makes COBRA, described in Chapter Eight, interesting and unique is that it uses Monte Carlo simulation software to calculate the probability of particular events or outcomes occurring. It is a means of modeling an uncertain future. Part of COBRA deals with bricks-and-mortar issues. If construction costs vary between $150 and $250 per square foot, for example, Monte Carlo simulation can demonstrate the probability that a new building might cost more than, say, $100 million or less than $80 million. For some companies, even a 5 percent chance that a building might cost more than $100 million would be an unacceptable risk. Assessing risk in this way is a step in the right direction, but it is insufficient. The focus remains almost exclusively on conventional financial analyses.

Equally important, as I've argued, is understanding how less tangible but no less important organizational and human resource factors—people issues—enter into the workspace equation. COBRA and the other tools described in Chapter Eight begin to address the fundamental dilemma of how one takes into consideration intangible factors that influence any workspace strategy's contribution to organizational performance. The answer, implicit throughout this book, lies in what might be called *uncommon sense*.

Questioning the Obvious Solution

Common sense suggests that decision makers select the conventional building located in the central business district. Uncommon sense says you should consider locating your technology staff or Web designers in converted factories and warehouses in light-industrial space. It's less expensive and is likely to be more attractive to the younger staff found in large numbers in technology units. Uncommon sense demands that we question the supposedly obvious solution.

Common sense says bringing everyone together under one roof significantly increases cross-unit collaboration and communication. Uncommon sense says the cost and effort of bringing divergent organizational units under one roof, whether a single large building or a corporate campus, has minimal impact on cross-functional interaction patterns beyond one's own floor, or outside of one's own department or team. Several uncommonsense corollaries stem from the limits of proximity. One is that once a team or department exceeds a single floor, it is unlikely to be worth a lot of effort and disruption to other groups to try to keep the splinter group close by. It makes more sense to divide the large unit into smaller subgroups and then co-locate each subgroup on the same floor. Keeping all groups on adjacent floors or even in the same building makes sense only if it doesn't cost much or disrupt other groups.

Uncommon sense takes many forms. As shown in Chapter Two, small-scale team-oriented office layouts with minimal or no panels or walls may reduce unwanted interruption and noise more than high-paneled cubicles do. Simple tools that sacrifice some accuracy for much greater speed can leave more time for deeper thinking and broader employee buy-in. Change management that targets development of informal change agents and information networks involves more people face-to-face and gives employees the right information on demand, when they want it, rather than relying on a few formal change agents and a predetermined schedule of presentations and workshops that may or may not address employee concerns at the right point in time. Uncommon sense says to take the time up front to do a culture audit, as described in Chapter Seven, because this is likely to reduce wasted time in journeys down dead-end paths later in the project.

A Few Good Rules

Unlimited choice is confusing; variation within a framework is liberating. As Chapter One argued, offices are physical artifacts reflecting ideas about how to conduct work-life. They are an invention, and a stage on which we play out the daily rituals of every-day work life. These rituals take myriad forms: talking on the telephone, gossiping over a cup of coffee, reading a report, hashing out a presentation with a colleague, and a thousand other behaviors. Individually, these daily rituals are simple; we don't spend much time thinking about or planning for them. But when played out by dozens if not hundreds or thousands of people they form a dense web of interdependent actions and relationships. On the surface, things may look disorderly, chaotic, disconnected. Underneath, more often there is a rhythm, a discernible pattern, and an internal logic.

Offices reflect not so much our experienced, lived-in world of work as the imagined social order, the order desired if not always achieved. How we capture and talk about our underlying social models shapes the physical form of the office and challenges our commonsense views of what the office is or can be.

The best offices I have seen were built on the premise of a few good rules. They might be evident in a single furniture system, same-size offices, and a consistent budget for furnishing a group common area. Decisions about how to allocate the budget were under the control of those employees who occupied a given area. Like British rowhouses with small front gardens, no two commons areas were fitted out identically. Few offices had the exact same complement of furniture arranged in the same way, but the office footprint, like rowhouses, was identical.

Fearing disorder, and having no strong culture to guide behavior, the common-sense impulse is to impose a barrage of restrictive policies and practices. But an overly detailed and prescriptive approach is suffocating and ultimately ineffective. What's needed instead is more of a "consolidated social agenda" embodying a coherent set of working principles for workspace performance. The ten principles given here offer such an approach.

Rule 1: Use Metaphors to Reinvent the Office

City planners, architects, and urban sociologists describe cities in metaphors. Metaphors are important because they shape the nature of our physical interventions in our environment. As city planner Spiro Kostos writes in reference to the form of cities: "If the city is a machine that must function efficiently, it is subject to obsoles-cence, and needs constant tuning and updating. If the city is an organism, and we speak of cells and arteries, it can become pathological, and interventions to correct the diseased form will be in the nature of surgery."[1]

What metaphors do we use to describe the office or workplace, and what ac-tions does the metaphor suggest? If the workplace is a *cafeteria*, shouldn't it provide a variety of menu items (offices, workstations, break areas) that customers' (employees) value? The office menu, like the restaurant menu, is likely to vary over time as cus-tomer tastes shift, and it will also vary from locale to locale. If the office is a *machine* that must function efficiently, predictably, and consistently in what it produces, doesn't it regular routine maintenance? Everything needs to be kept in its original, mint condition. If the places where we work are a *garden*, then shouldn't we understand how the systems and subsystems are nourished and interact as a dynamic ecosystem, and how changes in one part of the system will affect changes in other parts? Each metaphor implies actions, policies, rules, and values.

Rule 2: Find Order in Variety and Choice

One of the most enduring and fundamental organizational dilemmas concerns man-aging the relationship between order and disorder, or variety and choice. With the ex-ception of a place like a prison, we value the extreme of neither. We want both. We want things to be under control, but not stifling. We want to feel part of a group with-out sacrificing our individuality. We want variety but not chaos. Using the word *disor-der* as the counterpoint to *order* clouds the debate. If we substitute *variation* or *diversity* for *disorder,* both ends of the continuum become positives. Contrary to commonsense notions, order and diversity do not exist as opposing ends of a continuum. They com-plement each other.

Writing about cities, Kostos notes the apparent contradiction or disjuncture between rigid grid layouts and the variability, if not disorder, of the city as it is experienced. There is in fact irregularity in a strict plan: "Even when buildings are marshaled like troops along the lines of an urban grid, the degree of animation in their mass and, more essentially, variable height can result in picturesque formations believed to be congenital to the unplanned city. Manhattan's inflexible grid dissipates above ground into compilations that can range from the miscellaneous to the fantastic."[2] Order and variety each places a limit, perhaps inadvertently, on the other, so that neither dominates and both persist. In a way, it is an expression of a golden rule, finding a balance that controls extremism in the service of diversity.

Rule 3: Build Culture, Not Bureaucracy

In a world of constant organizational restructuring from mergers and acquisitions, downsizing, and explosive growth, all looked over by a parade of executives, few organizations live by a consistent set of values and expectations. As recently as fifty years ago this was less true. Then, there was greater acceptance of the social order and structure of the office. There were bosses and supervisors, staff and management, people in the trenches and people responsible for telling them what to do. It was a military model shaped by Max Weber's bureaucracy and Frederick Taylor's scientific management. Clear lines of authority, distinct specializations, and highly defined roles infused the social system. The idea that every employee, from raw recruit to CEO, is an "associate" or has no title at all was as foreign as the idea of a British general dressing for success with a decorated loincloth. So too was the idea of barrier-free team environments intended to promote interaction, or project teams working closely together electronically while geographically distributed across the globe.

Creating a rule for every organizational and workspace contingency employs many people for long periods of time, but it rarely works. Procedural manuals that detail every facet of building design from the desk to the fire safety sprinkler system collapse of their own weight and the collective disinterest on the part of all but those who created them. In contrast, having a few broad rules of the road means that within those rules *everything else* becomes possible. How, when, and where people work doesn't have to be micromanaged. A facility planner or interior designer doesn't need to specify the location of every storage cabinet and work surface within a team's area or an individual's workstation. Less energy, time, and money are needed than in erecting, monitoring, and enforcing a bureaucratic infrastructure. More time and effort are needed to identify and communicate the few operating principles and cultural values within which choice and variety can flourish. Diversity *and* order act as a natural limitation (and opportunity) to the other.

Rule 4: Exploit Uncertainty

Le Corbusier, the brilliant Swiss architect, championed a strict architectural order. In his 1924 book on urbanism Le Corbusier wrote that the pack-donkey "meanders along, meditates a little in his scatter-brained and distracted fashion; he zigzags in order to avoid the larger stones, or to ease the climb, or to gain a little shade; he takes the line of least resistance."[3] Le Corbusier abhorred such meanderings and viewed them as reflecting the absence of goals and a clear sense of direction. It's a commonsense idea. Uncommon sense suggests that following the less direct path may prove surprisingly beneficial.

Fritz Steele and I introduced the concept of "functional inconvenience" in *Workplace by Design* to capture the uncommonsense idea that deliberately planning for apparent inefficiency in the layout and design of circulation routes within an office promoted business effectiveness by increasing opportunities for serendipitous social contact and opportunistic learning.[4] There are, of course, times when we want to take a straight line; but at many other times the journey itself is what counts. GPS directional systems in cars capture this perfectly when they ask if you want the fastest route, the most scenic route, or the shortest route. It all depends. This is quite a different proposition from the view that anyone who values the journey as much as the destination is a jackass! We don't have to make strict choices between efficiency and effectiveness, or straight and meandering journeys. We need to extract the benefits of each.

Good workspace design emerges and evolves from thousands of decisions taken over time not just about the physical nature of the space but how it is allocated, used, managed, and adapted. These myriad decisions, reflecting images of work and workers, of what it means to be professional and businesslike, efficient and effective, cumulatively create the character of the space and determine its value over time. Strategies built on workspace diversity and variety are a much richer defense against the chronic uncertainty that Le Corbusier abhorred than are rigid rules that, under pressure, either take enormous effort to maintain or collapse of their own weight. Some elements of these strategies involve the physical environment—for example, highly adaptable environments like that found in the German company Igus described in Chapter Four, in which departments and activities can be relocated within a building quickly. Some involve corporate policies and practices about how space is used and allocated—for example, fewer codified rules and written policies. Sustainable ecologies are elastic. They evolve over time in response to changing conditions inside and outside the organization.

Rule 5: Pay Attention to the Backstage Office

In Western offices we pay more attention to the public character of the office, the front stage, than we do to the private backstage areas. Ornate, multistory lobbies with polished granite and rosewood grace the portal to backstage rabbit warrens built from densely packed identical work stations. Dutch architect Herman Hertzberger took a completely different approach when he designed the headquarters building for the Centraal Beheer insurance company in the Netherlands more than thirty years ago. The approach still resonates.

Hertzberger's building emphasized social neighborhoods shaped and regulated by the stacking and placement of room-sized cubes. These cubes generated a rigid building structure around human-scale rooms that encouraged employees to make the space their own by personalizing it with plants and how they arranged the furniture and used the space. The shaping of the building occurred both before and after occupancy. The structurally rigid cubes made it impossible to create huge standardized and uniform open plan knowledge farms. The building form itself generated the few good rules for maintaining an essentially inviolate human-scale spatial organization that could evolve over time. Coffee bars with free high-quality coffee distributed liberally throughout the building acted as neighborhood centers. Escalators and open stairs (not hidden fire stairs or an elevator) were the town's byways, making visual contact likely as one moved around the building carrying out the daily routine.

Conspicuous on architect's drawings and prominent in their presentations, the social spaces of the corporation are often more place markers for future growth than any commitment to a commonweal or deep belief in the value of conversation and communication for long-term corporate success. As the employee population swells, the sofas, easy chairs, and café-style barstools disappear under the rising tide of workstations needed to accommodate the expanding headcount. Costs and the need for space are tangible. Social capital, and the role it plays in the flow of ideas and information, is intangible. Under pressures for growth, efficiency and expediency bubble to the surface like gas under pressure.

Rule 6: Be Clear About the Organizational Objective

Too often managers are drawn to what is easy and efficient rather than what is right and effective. Robert Sommer, a pioneer in understanding how microdesign features such as furniture placement and room design influence interaction and behavioral patterns (a field of study he called "small group ecology"), captured this perfectly in his studies of mental institutions.[5] Sommer describes how the layout of large dayrooms in mental hospitals, in which all the chairs were pushed to the perimeter, was governed by the janitors' desire to wheel around their cleaning machines with minimum interference. The prime purpose of the institution, to improve social relations, was undermined by janitorial convenience.

Uncommon sense suggests that efficiency can spawn effectiveness and improve morale if it takes the form of simple rules that generate considerable opportunities for variety and choice. When my department at Cornell was relocated to another part of our college's building, we wanted to use the opportunity to replace furniture that had been around for a quarter century or more with something more modern. Steelcase was kind enough to offer us an attractive price on its products. But rather than the chair, or dean, or director of facilities sitting down with Steelcase and selecting the furniture, every faculty in the department was given the same furniture budget. Faculty could spend their allocation on any Steelcase product or furniture line they liked. That budget ceiling defined the few good rules. I wanted six comfortable ergonomic conference chairs and an attractive conference table; someone else wanted an integrated work surface and storage system. Those wanting wood surfaces got them but weren't able to order as many file cabinets as someone who chose a laminate product. We all chose something different. The process was fair, engaging, and motivating.

Rule 7: Focus on the System

The interdependence that constitutes the reality of every living system makes it impossible to understand, let alone improve, organizational performance by examining or changing any single facet, component, or element of the overall workspace system. It is the overall pattern that counts, not the individual element or facet. Knowing that a company has the best information technology, human resource practices, physical design, and manufacturing process does not predict the long-term success of the organization. Xerox is the poster child for the failure to capitalize on one of the greatest inventions of the twentieth century, the object-oriented language developed by researchers at Xerox PARC (the Palo Alto Research Center), led by David Kay. Not knowing how to market the invention, it languished at Xerox, only to be picked up and commercialized brilliantly at Apple, to change forever how we interacted with our computers. The same applies to the planning, design, and management of workspace. Herman Miller's Ergon chair is superb. It contributes to employee comfort and satisfaction, but by itself it doesn't transform a mediocre employee into a high performer. Neither does a well-designed desk, or just the right location for the office building. High performance requires alignment of all the elements of the work system, from design, space, and technology to the formal and informal management policies, practices, and values that define the corporate culture.

Rule 8: Promote Differentiation and Choice

Outside the workplace, most of us seek out and modify where we live within the constraints of our own bank balance and imagination. Drive around your neighborhood and look at the small, even subtle changes your neighbors have made to the exterior of often virtually identical homes. Shutters in a kaleidoscope of colors, patios, converted garages, and gardens of every conceivable size and shape transform an essentially uniform infrastructure into an idiosyncratic place. It is this constant embellishment that over time gives neighborhoods their charm and adds resale value to the houses in them. This kind of design variation is small but not trivial. It makes a difference. Like blades of grass growing in the cracks of concrete, the urge to claim some small sense of personal identity is irrepressible.

Too often, companies discourage this kind of differentiation, viewing it as Pandora's box, raising the lid on an anything-goes mentality and undermining the sense of a single, strong corporate brand. Yet manufacturers have come to understand the value of giving consumers real choice in selecting and shaping the products they buy. This involves telling the vendor what we want, and getting it quickly and at a reasonable price. Mass customization makes possible manufacturing one unit of a hundred thousand different things, whether Levi's jeans or Dell computers, rather than a hundred thousand units of the same thing.

In practice, whether buying a car or a computer, we select from a predetermined palate of choices. The car comes in ten, not a hundred, colors. The computer has three choices for memory size, not fifty. Having only a few options, but the right ones, reduces build time and cost. You don't need unlimited choices; you need ones that people care about. Economies of scale disappear quickly if you manufacture ten thousand computers that consumers don't want to buy.

In the context of workspace strategy, Union Carbide learned this almost twenty years ago when it planned its new world headquarters in Danbury, Connecticut. Seeking variety in its offices, the company offered a choice of fifteen distinct office layouts, each of which came in two distinct color schemes. Every one of the three thousand employees who moved from midtown Manhattan to the Danbury office chose which of those thirty office options he or she wanted. It turned out that between five and ten options accounted for 80 percent of the choices. Workspace consultant Cindy Froggatt, then a graduate student at Cornell, found in her research the highest satisfaction level we had ever seen reported for an office environment. Not only was satisfaction high, but one uncommonsense consequence of more choice was that the cost of furnishing the offices themselves, despite their executive look with carpets and wood furniture, was no more than what standard contract systems furniture would have cost.

Companies such as Union Carbide in the early 1980s and SAS (a leader in business analytic software and services) in North Carolina today attract, retain, and motivate their employees at an enviable level by paying attention to what environmental psychologist John Zeisel called the "nonpaying customer": the employee. Consideration of initial cost and administrative ease and residual value doesn't disappear, but the importance is balanced against the possibility of implementing uncommonsense solutions that contribute value over the long run because they are grounded in a deep understanding of the people who actually use the space.

Rule 9: Encourage Flexible Work Patterns

Another way of thinking about requisite or sufficient variety, in addition to product modification and customization, is in the variety of settings inside and outside the office available for employees to use and the degree of flexibility in how they are used and work gets done. Here, meaningful differentiation puts an arrow in the heart of the idea of a nine-to-five workday spent sitting at a single assigned desk. Dot coms, for all their other failings, got this right. Shaggy-looking computer programmers came into the office whenever they wanted and then stayed until one or two in the morning. Performance wasn't confused with good citizenship, coming to work early or on time, and going home at a prescribed time. It was getting good work done in a timely manner. Where and when one worked was a matter of choice, not corporate dictate. If you observe how people actually work, you will see that many people have worked this way for a long time. But the image of work as fixed in space and time persists, even as standardized time-activity patterns are giving way to customized ones.

Rule 10: Rethink What Constitutes Professionalism

Common sense suggests that the greatest barrier to functional diversity is the cost and effort to plan, design, and operate settings that are not uniform, and to manage people whose whereabouts cannot be monitored easily. In fact, the real point of resistance is more cultural than technical or functional. It is deeply held views of what it means to be professional.

Culture's iron fist expresses itself in all manner of enterprise. English farmers on the Sussex Downs resist leaving corners and edges of their fields unplowed. Leaving ragged edges unplowed costs nothing and allows birds like the corn bunting to nest in the tufts of grass and trees that grow in little protected thickets. But it looks untidy to farmers who take pride in how they maintain their fields. Unplowed corners are seen as a sign of being unprofessional and lazy. So plowed they are. Managers who have grown up with a military model of management, in which control and order are paramount, are likely to see any highly diverse environment the same way a Sussex farmer views an unplowed corner of a field: as untidy, out of control, and evidence of a lack of professionalism. Professional pride can be the innovative workspace's enemy, or its greatest ally. Images of what it means to be professional are deeply ingrained. But if changed, that hardiness becomes an asset.

The truth of this was brought home to me in the early 1990s when I visited DEC and SOL in Finland, two companies I continue to use as examples despite their having been around for more than a decade because they are simply two of the most innovative and productive offices I have ever known. They were lively, vital places, full of activity and energy. What surprised me was that in both cases the client had to fire well-respected architectural firms in the quest to develop an unconventional and highly productive workspace. The architects simply could not fathom a workspace that, in the case of SOL, had a kind of frumpy residential feel to it. DEC, with its inexpensive swing sets, porch furniture, and lazy-boy recliner chairs, had a more sophisticated but still residential character. Neither place projected the kind of crisp, subdued, and understated character associated with professional offices just about everywhere.

Developed within a consistent and coherent framework of strategic workspace principles, choice and variety, like the other principles of effective workspace design, make uncommon sense. The challenge is to find the right level of functional diversity. It is not about variety for variety's sake. The business value of the right amount and type of choice derives from its ability to achieve what often appear to be contradictory goals: cost reduction, improved employee morale, greater organizational flexibility, and strong corporate branding. The answer is not for companies to blindly imitate a DEC Finland, SOL, or IDEO. It is to understand at a sufficiently deep level the nature of the work processes, corporate culture, labor demographics, and marketplace to be able to be truly inventive.

Such planning and design processes will take more time than stamping out the same workplace design the company has used for the past decade. The fact that the company has not imploded during this time and may have even prospered can mask what it might have achieved. I can drive a car with one cylinder stuck. It will go forward. But its performance bears no resemblance to the same car's performance when all cylinders are firing. The result of considering uncommon workspace strategies is not simply workspace that is attractive or cost-efficient. It is space that, like all good investments, actually performs well and adds value over the long run.

Implications for Practice

- One size doesn't fit all. Celebrate diversity in how individuals and units function; don't fear or try to mask it.
- Don't confuse "equity" with everyone having the same thing. Think of it as everyone within a common category having access to resources of comparable value.
- Create opportunities for choice, the ability to influence aspects of the workplace, at every level of the organization, right down to the team and individual. But recognize that choice need not be unlimited. Provide sufficient choice to mark meaningful distinctions, ones that people actually care about.
- Involve a cross-section of the organization in developing and communicating the framework, the few good rules (inside and outside the organization) within which variation can occur so that there is a shared understanding of why some aspects of the workplace are standardized and uniform and others are allowed to vary.

REFERENCES

Introduction

1. Becker, F., and Steele, F. *Workplace by Design: Mapping the High-Performance Workscape*. San Francisco: Jossey-Bass, 1995.
2. Pfeffer, J., and Sutton, R. I. *The Knowing-Doing Gap: How Smart Companies Turn Knowledge into Action*. Boston: Harvard Business School Press, 2000.

Chapter One: The Office as Invention

1. Drucker, P. "The Future That Has Already Happened." *Harvard Business Review,* 1997, *75*(5), 20–23.
2. Duffy, F. "Design and Facilities Management in a Time of Change." *Facilities,* 2000, *18*(10), 371–375.
3. Kelley, T. *The Art of Innovation*. New York: HarperCollins Business, 2002.
4. Naisbitt, J., and Aburdene, P. *Megatrends 2000: Ten New Directions for the 1990s*. New York: Morrow, 1990.

Chapter Two: Knowledge Networks

1. Krebs, V. "Knowledge Networks—Mapping and Measuring Knowledge Creation and Re-Use." 2002. (www.orgnet.com/IHRIM.html)

2. Taylor, F. *The Principles of Scientific Management.* New York: HarperCollins, 1911.

3. Yukl, G. *Leadership in Organizations.* (4th ed.) Upper Saddle River, N.J.: Prentice Hall, 1998.

4. Mascitelli, R. "From Experience: Harnessing Tacit Knowledge to Achieve Breakthrough Innovation." *Journal of Product Innovation Management,* 2000, *17,* 179.

5. Brown, J. S., and Duguid, P. "Organizational Learning and Communities of Practice: Toward a Unified View of Working, Learning, and Innovation." *Organization Science, 2*(1), 1991, 40–58.

6. Lave, J., and Wenger, E. *Situated Learning: Legitimate Peripheral Participation.* New York: Cambridge University Press, 1993.

7. Feldman, M. S. "Electronic Mail and Weak Ties in Organizations." *Office: Technology and People,* 1987, *3,* 103.

8. Becker, F., and Sims, W. *Offices That Work: Balancing Communication, Flexibility, and Cost.* Ithaca, N.Y.: International Workplace Studies Program, Cornell University, 2001, p. 22.

9. International Facility Management Association. *Facility Management Practices: Research Report no. 16.* Houston: International Facility Management Association, 1996.

10. Kraut, R. E., Fish, R. E., Root, R., and Chalfonte, B. "Informal Communication in Organizations: Form, Function, and Technology." In S. Oskamp and S. Spacapan (eds.), *People's Reactions to Technology in Factories, Offices, and Aerospace.* Thousand Oaks, Calif.: Sage, 1990.

11. Kraut, R. E., Galegher, J., and Egido, C. "Relationships and Tasks in Scientific Research Collaborations." In I. Grief (ed.), *Computer-Supported Cooperative Work: A Book of Readings.* San Mateo, Calif.: Morgan Kaufman, 1988.

12. Backhouse, A., and Drew, P. "The Design Implications of Social Interaction in a Workplace Setting." *Environment and Planning B: Planning and Design,* 1992, *19,* 573–584.

13. Becker and Sims (2001).

14. Becker and Sims (2001), p. 14.

15. Becker and Sims (2001), p. 15.

16. Evans, G. "Stress and Open Office Noise." *Journal of Applied Psychology,* 2000, *8*(5), 779.

17. Brill, M., Keable, E., and Fabinlak, J. "The Myth of the Open Plan." *Journal of Design and Management,* 2000, *19,* 36.

18. Becker and Sims (2001), p. 16.

19. Teasley, S. D., Covi, L. A., Krishnan, M. S., and Olson, J. S. "Rapid Software Development Through Team Collocation." *IEEE Transactions in Software Engineering,* 2002, *28*(7), 671–681.

Chapter Three: Co-Location

1. Allen, T. *The Flow of Technology.* Cambridge, Mass.: MIT Press, 1976.

2. Kraut, Fish, Root, and Chalfonte (1990); Kraut, Galegher, and Egido (1988).

3. Grieshop, J., and Sommer, R. "Building Synergy Among A&ES Special Programs." (Unpublished report.) Davis: Community Development Program, University of California, 1990.

4. Becker, F., Sims, W., and Schoss, J. *Interaction, Identity and Collocation: What Value Is a Corporate Campus?* Ithaca, N.Y.: International Workplace Studies Program, Cornell University, 2002.

Chapter Four: The Right Size

1. Potter, D. V. "Scale Matters." *Across the Board*, 2000, *37*(7), 36–40.
2. Molloy, J. T. *Dress for Success*. New York: P. H. Wyden, 1975.
3. Reason, T. "Shareware?" *CFO*, Sept. 2000, pp. 101–108.
4. Reason (2000).
5. Reason (2000).
6. Duany, A., and Plater-Zyberk, E. "The Neighborhood, the District and the Corridor." In P. Katz (ed.), *The New Urbanism: Toward an Architecture of Community*. New York: McGraw-Hill, 1994.
7. Duany and Plater-Zyberk (1994), p. xx.
8. Bressi, T. W. "Planning the American Dream." In P. Katz (ed.), *The New Urbanism: Toward an Architecture of Community*. New York: McGraw-Hill, 1994, p. xxvi.
9. Gladwell, M. *The Tipping Point: How Little Things Can Make a Big Difference*. New York: Little, Brown, 2000.
10. Gladwell (2000), pp. 178–179.
11. Maxwell, L. E. "Home and School Density Effects on Elementary School Children: The Role of Spatial Density." *Environment and Behavior*, 2003, *35*(4), 566–578.
12. Gladwell (2000), p. 184.

Chapter Five: Mobility

1. Wiesenfeld, B. M., and Raghuram, S. "Communication Patterns as Determinants of Organizational Identification in a Virtual Organization." *Organization Science*, 1999, *10*(8), 1–18.
2. "Borders Are So 20th Century." *Business Week*, Sept. 2004, 72–73.
3. Watson-Manheim, M. B., and Belanger, F. "Support for Communication-Based Work Processes in Virtual Work." *e-Service Journal*, 2002, pp. 61–82.
4. Kelley (2002).
5. Froggatt, C. *Work Naked: Eight Essential Principles for Peak Performance in the Virtual Workplace*. San Francisco: Jossey-Bass, 2001.
6. Froggatt (2001).
7. Wiesenfeld and Raghuram (1999).

Chapter Six: Flexibility

1. Lyne, J. "Real Estate and the Web: IDRC Probes the Big Questions." *Site Selection*, Sept. 2000, pp. 798–802.
2. Gaudreau, B. "Managing Real Estate at the Speed of Change." *Corporate Real Estate Leader*, 2003, *2*(5), 32–33.
3. Becker, F., and Sims, R. *Managing Uncertainty: Portfolio Strategies for Dynamic Organizations*. Ithaca, N.Y.: International Workplace Studies Program, Cornell University, 2001.
4. Becker and Sims, *Managing Uncertainty* (2001).
5. Becker and Sims, *Managing Uncertainty* (2001).

6. Lerch, K. "The 'Surge' Complex." *Facilities Design and Management,* Apr. 2000, pp. 38–39.

7. Lerch (2000), p. 39.

8. Becker and Sims, *Managing Uncertainty* (2001).

9. Pilon, L., and Gee, L. "Herman Miller's MarketPlace Building: Gold LEED Rating, Below Norm Costs, and a Successful Partnership." *Corporate Real Estate Leader,* 2003, *2*(5), 20ff.

10. Becker, F. D., and Poe, D. "The Effect of User-Generated Design Modification in a General Hospital." *Journal of Nonverbal Behavior,* 1980, *4,* 195–218.

Chapter Seven: Getting Started

1. Beinhocker, E. D. "Robust Adaptive Strategies." *Sloan Management Review,* 1999, *40*(3), 95–106; Pascale, R. T. "Surfing the Edge of Chaos." *Sloan Management Review,* 1999, *40*(3), 83–94.

Chapter Eight: Workspace Planning Tools

1. Hendriks, L. "Customers in Sight: Supporting Corporate Accommodation Decisions with Real Estate Data." *Journal of Corporate Real Estate,* 2002, *4*(3), 275–296.

2. Schriefer, A., and Ganesh, J. "Putting Corporate Real Estate Executives in the Driver's Seat: Information Technology Tools Enable New Possibilities." *Journal of Corporate Real Estate,* 2002, *4*(3), 227–236.

3. Becker, F., and Pearce, A. "Considering Corporate Real Estate and Human Resource Factors in an Integrated Cost Model." *Journal of Corporate Real Estate,* 2003, *5*(3), 221–242.

Chapter Ten: Managing Workspace Change

1. Becker, F., Tennessen, C., and Dahl, L. *Managing Workplace Change.* Ithaca, N.Y.: International Workplace Studies Program, Cornell University, 1997.

2. Pfeffer and Sutton (2000).

3. Becker and Pearce (2003).

Chapter Eleven: Uncommon Sense

1. Kostos, S. *The City Shaped: Urban Patterns and Meanings Through History.* Boston: Bulfinch Press, 1991, p. 16.

2. Kostos (1991), p. 44.

3. Kostos (1991), p. 95.

4. Becker and Steele (1995).

5. Sommer, R. *Personal Space: The Behavioral Basis of Design.* Reading, Mass.: Addison-Wesley, 1969.

THE AUTHOR

Franklin Becker is chair of the Department of Design and Environmental Analysis and Director of the International Workplace Studies Program (IWSP) at Cornell University. At Cornell University in 1980 he founded, with William Sims, the first Facility Planning and Management degree program in the world. With groundbreaking research on alternative officing, his work in organizational ecology led to development of the concept of the integrated workplace strategy, in which organizational performance is viewed as being forged by the interaction of space, culture, technology, demographics, and work processes. In addition to his academic responsibilities, Becker is president of IDEAworks, a management consulting firm offering a range of services related to planning, designing, evaluating, and managing workspace. He has conducted research, lectured, and consulted in England, Canada, Europe, Japan, Australia, and New Zealand as well as the United States. He is the author of five books, among them *Workplace by Design: Mapping the High-Performance Workscape* (with Fritz Steele, Jossey-Bass, 1995).

Index